ESTHER:
courage in crisis

A radiant queen's courageous response
can give you boldness to meet your
times of stress.

MARGARET HESS

This book is designed for your personal
reading pleasure and profit. It is also
designed for group study. A leader's guide
with helps and hints for teachers and
visual aids (Victor Multiuse Transparency
Masters) is available from your local book-
store or from the publisher at $2.95.

VICTOR BOOKS

a division of SP Publications, Inc.

WHEATON. ILLINOIS 60187

Offices also in Fullerton, California • Whitby, Ontario, Canada • Amersham on the Hill, Bucks, England

D0250400

Second printing, 1980

Unless otherwise noted, all Scripture quotations are from the King James Version. Other versions used are the *New American Standard Version* (NASB) © 1960, 1962, 1963, 1968, 1971, 1972, 1973, the Lockman Foundation, La Habra, California; *The Amplified Bible* (AMP) © 1965 Zondervan Publishing House, Grand Rapids, Michigan; the *New International Version* (NIV) © 1978 by New York International Bible Society; *The New Berkeley Version* (BERK) © 1969 by the Zondervan Publishing House; *The Holy Bible: An American Translation* by William F. Beck (BECK) © Mrs. William F. Beck, 1976.

Recommended Dewey Decimal Classification: 222.9 or 229.27
Suggested subject heading: ESTHER

Library of Congress Catalog Card Number: 79-55321
ISBN: 0-88207-216-1

VICTOR BOOKS
A division of SP Publications, Inc.
P.O. Box 1825 • Wheaton, Illinois 60187

WHAT OTHERS SAY . . .

BS41

Margaret Hess has given us an intimate insight into the lives of the book's characters and makes the lessons of Esther very practical for our personal lives, our churches, and our everyday struggles with evil as well as the enjoyment of our successes. The book is valuable for Bible study by groups because there are many opportunities for spin offs in thinking whereby everyone can enter in with personal profit."

Louis Goldberg, Th.D.
Professor of Theology and Jewish Studies
Moody Bible Institute
Chicago, Illinois

"I like the whole approach. I like the flow of thought and language. I like the little personal things."

Rabbi Martin D. Gordon
The Livonia Jewish Congregation
Livonia, Michigan

"Family physicians are very much aware of the problems in living which stress individuals and families today. Margaret Hess has given some sound advice for coping with these kinds of problems through a delightful and effective study of the Old Testament Book of Esther. She points out that God has a plan for every life, and successful living involves appropriate relationships with God, self, and others."

Murray N. Deighton, M.D.
Chairman
Department of Family Practice
Providence Hospital
Southfield, Michigan

Contents

Appreciation

To my husband, Bartlett L. Hess, Ph.D. in history, Bible expositor, and pastor. He helped with the bibliography, gave constant inspiration and encouragement, read and criticized the manuscript chapter by chapter.

.To Marilynn Adams for knowledgeable typing and retyping.

Foreword

Imagine—a book of the Bible begins with life in a harem. More is said about that life than is recorded in any other ancient writing. And the heroine of the story becomes part of the harem.

The Book of Esther, at first glance, seems a strange account to find in the Bible. The name of God is not mentioned. Nothing is said about the Law of God, the temple, or Jewish worship. Prayer isn't referred to. No rules are laid down for living, and no morals are drawn from the story. The whole thing looks like a strictly secular narrative. At first glance.

A deeper look transforms the Book of Esther into a tremendous spiritual experience. You see exactly how God works in history, and how He works in your life.

You probably always knew, or suspected, that God *created* the universe. The Book of Esther demonstrates how He *maintains* and *controls* life on our planet. He's in command of events. Yet God doesn't interfere with the free will He's given you. Bad people and good make their own decisions.

Behind the action taking place on life's stage, we sense God behind the scenes as Director. He's the real Hero of the Book. He works through people to bring about His objectives—even through their evil schemings and selfish mistakes. There is no need to maneuver to favorably present any human personality in Esther.

Filmy curtains of rationalizing, hung up by so many commentators, can be pulled aside. The actions of some colorful individuals can be looked at under the bright lights of honesty.

Actions and their results in the Book of Esther reveal much about life. You will see good examples to follow, bad examples to avoid, good and evil bound up together, and people facing difficult choices.

Do you ever wonder if the Almighty concerns Himself with your life? Do you wish to find your place in God's plan? The Book of Esther will show you how.

Introduction

Writers on the Book of Esther cope with its "difficulties" in various ways.

Many back off from an historical interpretation entirely by taking off into strange allegories. Esther becomes the church, the Holy Spirit, Christ, the Virgin Mary, the Gentiles. Mordecai and Ahasuerus become whatever the writer wants to make them. You could hunt through a whole attic of odds and ends of ideas about Esther without discovering any general agreement on figurative meanings. So you throw out allegories for the Book of Esther as you throw out most remedies for the common cold. The multitude of suggestions proves none are specific.

The Greek translators several centuries before Christ added to the Hebrew text to make Esther and Mordecai look better. They also added some glaring historical inaccuracies. Only the original Hebrew text checks out historically and archeologically.

Josephus, the Jewish historian from the time of Paul, drew material from the inaccurate Greek translation (the Septuagint). Commentators throughout the centuries copied from both, and from each other.

If we recognize God as the real Hero behind the Book of Esther, we feel no embarrassment about the basic Hebrew text. It was recognized in the time of Christ as part of Scripture, to which He gave His word of approval.

We're relieved of any obligation to defend Esther's going into a pagan king's harem. We need not argue that Mordecai acted rightly in refusing to bow down to Haman or to instruct Esther to cover up her Jewishness. We don't have to defend the Jews for killing 75,000 Persians.

God worked through the lives of Ahasuerus, Mordecai, Esther, and even Haman to evidence Himself in the world. He put it all together.

We see the Book of Esther as a microcosm of the Jewish experience repeated over and over again throughout history up to the present day.

We understand our world better for knowing the Book of Esther. We see afresh God at work all around us.

1
Have You Shared in Life's Feasts?

How would you like to attend banquets and listen to speeches for six months? Sometimes three hours seem too long.

Long ago, in ancient Persia, lived a king who called all the important people together from his empire. He wanted to demonstrate, by the magnificence of his feasts, what a great man he was. You know how much it costs to put on one company dinner. Imagine providing six months of gormandizing for hundreds of people.

Yet the king, Ahasuerus, hadn't learned the first secret of hospitality—unselfishness. He invited those princes, officials, and army officers only because he wished to make an impression. He wanted to involve them in his project.

Why do you invite people to dinner? One young minister's wife had to learn the ABCs of hospitality the hard way. Her husband wanted her to entertain a group of callers at their home to show appreciation for their dedicated work.

"Oh," she groaned, "how can I? I have my Sunday-School class to teach and the children to take care of. I'll have to take a week off from studying to wax the floors and wash all the curtains. And then all that baking to do—it always takes a full week of hard work to get ready."

He looked around. "What's the matter with the house? It looks all right to me."

"But you can't invite people without getting ready for them. It's a matter of hospitality."

His eyes flashed. "That's not hospitality. That's selfish pride. Just invite them over. People will help you with the food."

Always before, by the time people arrived, she'd felt tense and exhausted and was unable to enjoy her guests. They knew it. Now she realized she'd mainly wanted to make an impression. She tried entertaining her husband's way and it worked. People really enjoyed themselves and she did too. True hospitality is simply sharing what you have and are without straining to impress.

The Bible exhorts us to hospitality: "Be hospitable to one another without complaint" (1 Peter 4:9, NASB; see also Luke 14:12-14; Rom. 12:13; 1 Tim. 3:2; Titus 1:7-8; Heb. 13:2).

Ahasuerus in many ways shows us how not to do it. The author of the Book of Esther mentioned Ahasuerus' feast for only one reason. What happened at the banquet cleared the way for Esther to become queen of the harem. The author, with a few deft strokes, sketched the setting for his account. He answered the questions of who (v. 1), where (v. 2), what, and when (v. 3). The Book of Esther comes alive only as we know where and when it took place.

"Now it took place in the days of Ahasuerus, the Ahasuerus who reigned from India to Ethiopia over 127 provinces" (1:1, NASB).

We're first introduced to the king of the harem, Ahasuerus, who put on the banquet. He reigned over the Persian empire at its height and was the most powerful monarch in the world up to that time. His empire extended over half the known world—from the part of India drained by the Indus River, to Ethiopia, south of Egypt.

We each have our area of power—a home; a schoolroom; an office; a group of friends; maybe a business, with employees; a church; an organization, small or large; a committee. Each of us is responsible to God for what we do with that power. We'll watch how Ahasuerus handled his power.

Who was Ahasuerus? Not long ago, archeologists began digging around in the ruins at Persepolis, Persia. They found many inscriptions, some in three languages. They positively identified Ahasuerus as the historical king Xerxes. The name of the son of Darius appeared as *Khshayarsha* in Persian. In the Babylonian column it appeared as *Adhashwerosh*, almost identical with the Hebrew form in the Book of Esther. In the parallel column in Greek, they read *Xerxes*. Translated into English, that's Ahasuerus.

You can easily read all about Xerxes in Herodotus' *History* (bks. 7—9). Of course to Herodotus, a Greek historian, Greece's triumph over Xerxes seemed the important thing about him. Therefore, he recounts in detail how Xerxes invaded Greece with an untrained horde representing his whole empire. Greece's army, small and well-disciplined, routed Xerxes' army at the Battle of Thermopolae. Greece's navy destroyed most of Xerxes' collection of ships at the Battle of Salamis. The rest went scurrying home.

You find in Herodotus so much about Xerxes as a person that you feel you know him. A sensual and capricious despot, only Xerxes could have acted the way Ahasuerus did in the Book of Esther.

Herodotus and the inscriptions discovered at Persepolis confirm that India and Ethiopia paid tribute to Xerxes. The 127 provinces that made up the empire were conquered nations. These provinces were combined into some 30 satrapies. The author of Esther brings out the vastness of Xerxes' power to enhance the miracle of God's deliverance of the Jews.

"Now it took place . . . ." (1:1, NASB)

The Book of Esther starts out with the Hebrew word *wayehi*. You find it as the first word in other historical books like Joshua, Judges, and 1 and 2 Samuel. Each of these continues the narrative of the preceding book.

Only the book of Esther tells us anything about what happened to the Jews in captivity who didn't return to Jerusalem after Cyrus issued his decree permitting their return in 536 B.C. We see God's providential care over His people during Xerxes' reign (485—465 B.C.), even when they lived outside their land. That care has continued throughout history.

"In those days when King Ahasuerus sat on his royal throne in the Shushan palace . . ." (1:2, BERK)

We encounter no difficulty in pinpointing Susa, Persia's capital. Persia became Iran in 1935. If you go to Iran, you can inspect the remains of Susa. It's a mound of ruins some 200 miles north of the Persian Gulf. Scholars identified the location in 1852, excavated in 1884-86, and again in 1946-51.

The author of Esther correctly distinguishes between the town of Susa and the palace or castle. The word translated "palace" or "capital" means literally "fortress." The town lay on the right bank of a wide river. Today only slight undulations of the plain mark the site of the town. They show it to have been seven miles around.

Across the river stood the fortified palace, on an acropolis 72 feet higher than the surrounding plain. It's two and one-half miles around. The finds verify descriptions in the Book of Esther down to the most minute details. When you get to know Susa, you also know the palace where Nehemiah served as cupbearer some 40 years later, to Artaxerxes, son of Xerxes (Neh. 2:1).

Persian kings spent only their winters in Susa. In summer Susa becomes unbearably hot. Strabo, a Greek geographer, said snakes and lizards trying to crawl across the streets were burned to death, and barley grains bounced like parched grains in the oven (Strabo 15. 3:10-11).

So Persian kings rotated the rest of the year among their palaces at Persepolis, Ecbatana, and Babylon. They moved the court to the plateau of Persepolis in the summer to cool off. I visited Persepolis in May and enjoyed the vast columns and magnificent carvings. You can see there the figure of Xerxes sculptured in stone in many reliefs on the walls of his palaces. But I found the heat even there so intense I could hardly stand it, and I wondered how the Persian Court found relief there.

At Susa as well as at Persepolis you can see the ground plan of once sumptuous buildings. Here the great Xerxes "*sat*." Among the Orientals, sitting was the official posture for kings and judges. Persian monuments always represent kings seated upon a lofty chair. Greek writers record that Persian kings traveled and even went into battle seated upon a throne. Herodotus describes Xerxes as watching the disastrous battle of Thermopylae from a throne (7. 212). Plutarch says the same of the disastrous sea battle near Salamis.

"In those days . . . "(1:2, BERK)

The author evidently wrote after Xerxes' reign ended. It's on looking back usually that we can see the total pattern of God's plan. At the time, events may look like a jigsaw puzzle that hasn't been put together. Yet God knows all the parts are there. Only afterward can we see the design.

The Book of Esther must have been written in the heart of Persia, by a person intimately acquainted with customs as well as scenery. He seems to have had access to Persian documents. He uses some purely Persian words such as *pur, bathshegan, akhashteranim* and *karpas.* Yet he must have been a Jew because he wrote in such excellent Hebrew. He shows intense Jewish nationalism. The Book of Esther contains no Greek words, so it couldn't have been written after the Greeks conquered Persia in 331 B.C.

"In the third year of his reign he gave a banquet for all his nobles and officials. The military leaders of Persia and Media, the princes, and the nobles of the provinces were present" (1:3, NIV).

Reading Herodotus, you even learn about some of the speeches given at that long, drawn-out banquet. He says Xerxes "called together an assembly of the noblest Persians to learn their opinions, and to lay before them his own designs" (7. 8). That happened in the third year of his reign, after he had subdued a rebellion in Egypt. To stir up enthusiasm and make levies for his march on Athens, Xerxes focused the empire's energies on devouring one little country. It looked easy.

Because our world is permeated with sin, the strong prey on the weak. The wolf pulls down the old moose. The lustful seduce the innocent. Scoundrels rob the naive. The powerful exploit the unprepared. An empire gobbles up a small nation.

But the story of Esther does not concern itself with Ahasuerus as a military man. We see him in the Book of Esther as the man who held power of life or death over Jews in the Persian Empire.

"He displayed the wealth of his regal glory and the costly glamour of his majesty for many days, for 180 days" (1:4, BERK).

Sometimes you're invited to a banquet because an organization wants to get money out of you. Occasionally, you learn that fact too late. If your host bragged on and on about his project and pinched you for funds—well, six months is a long time. Some writers suggest that officials of the provinces came and went for that period of time. We don't know. But if an autocrat like Xerxes invited you, it would come across as a command.

Xerxes expected everyone to encourage him in his adventure. He also expected each to contribute his quota of soldiers and ships or supplies. Only one man, according to Herodotus, showed enough courage to point out the foolhardiness of the project. But Xerxes had already invested two years in preparations. After the banqueting he would invest two more. Then he would start his march to Greece, accompanied by an army from all the provinces (Herodotus 7. 20).

"When those days were over, the king gave a banquet lasting seven days, in the enclosed park of the king's

palace, for all the people, high and low, who were in the
fortress city of Susa" (1:5, BECK).

Maybe 180 days represented all the time given to meetings and reckoning up resources for the invasion. Perhaps the real celebration was during the seven days. But
Xerxes did feed those people sumptuously for the whole
six months. The Hebrew term translated "banquet"
means a state banquet, at which time a lot of drinking
went on.

Xerxes included many in this week-long banquet,
without regard to rank: all his courtiers, members of the
royal household not hitherto included, as well as ambas-
sadors and representatives from the many countries of
his domain. We too need the cooperation of everyone,
important and unimportant, in accomplishing any big
project for church, school, home, or community. It's
only sensible to share privileges as well as responsibilities.

Xerxes needed everybody's help for tackling little
Greece! The Greeks had dared to affront his pride. They
alone, he thought, stood in the way of his overrunning all
Europe.

Archeologists have identified the garden where
Ahasuerus held his banquet in the ruins at Susa. The
courtyard paved with mosaic formed part of the park
surrounding the royal palace. The whole was enclosed
by walls.

"There were hangings of fine white cloth, of green and
of blue [cotton], fastened with cords of fine linen and
purple to silver rings or rods and marble pillars. The
couches of gold and silver rested on a (mosaic) pavement
of porphyry, white marble, mother-of-pearl, and (pre-
cious) colored stones" (1:6, AMP).

Even the vast halls of the palace could not contain so many guests. So workmen constructed tent-like hangings as protection from the sun. These awnings hung from silver rings or rods and from pillars. Remains of the pillars and mosaic have come to light. An inscription found at Susa lists the many rich stones and materials drawn from all over the empire for this palace. Skilled workmen of many nations contributed their artistry to the palace.

Orientals used couches instead of chairs at banquets. Some say the writer must have meant couches covered with gold or silver cloth. But Herodotus describes the plunder Xerxes left when his army fled Greece. They "found many tents richly adorned with furniture of gold and silver, many couches covered with plates of the same, and many golden bowls, goblets, and other drinking-vessels. On the carriages were bags containing silver and golden kettles; and the bodies of the slain furnished bracelets and chains, and scymitars with golden ornaments" (Herodotus 9. 80-83). Many artistically wrought golden vessels have come down to us from the time of the Persian empire.

"Wine was served in goblets of gold, each one different from the other, and the royal wine was abundant, in keeping with the king's liberality" (1:7, NIV).

Xerxes offered his guests all the wine they wanted. Imagine the state of their heads, stomachs, and spirits as the week progressed. Feasting must have become less and less enjoyable. Even Epicureans, who lived for pleasure, urged temperance as a necessary means to pleasure. You can only enjoy to the utmost by restraining yourself from surfeit. Americans have discovered they dare not eat all they can afford to buy.

"And the drinking was according to the law; none did compel: for so the king had appointed to all the officers of his house, that they should do according to every man's pleasure" (1:8, NASB).

Such freedom in drinking departed from the norm. Ancient Persians are described by Herodotus and others as heavy drinkers. However, during the feast this pagan king showed more sense than many modern hosts and hostesses. Said the prophet Habbakkuk, "Woe to him who gives drink to his neighbors, pouring it from the wineskin till they are drunk, so that he can gaze on their naked bodies" (Hab. 2:15, NIV).

Sometimes hostesses press food and drink upon guests. True hospitality offers, but stops short of pushing. Guests don't appreciate a hostess who manipulates them into overindulging.

A commentator of a past century pointed out that Xerxes' banquet appealed to all five senses: sight and touch, in the luxurious furnishings; smell, in the delicate odors of flowers in the garden; taste, in the food and drink. Music was not provided for the hearing, he said, because taste in music differs. You cannot shut it out if you don't like it. But in the end even hearing was gratified because they listened to each person's desires in his drinking.

God provides for us daily far more lavish delights than any Xerxes could afford: the beauties of forest, field, and stream; good food to eat, and hunger to spice it with; music of our own choosing, in nature or from the music man can produce.

The most powerful monarch in the world had gathered all the riches man could imagine. Xerxes, at this moment, possessed all the world could offer—power, wealth, pleasure, and at least a semblance of popularity.

Herodotus said Xerxes even possessed good looks. Among all the myriads of his army, Xerxes excelled in stature and beauty (7.187). But did it all add up to happiness? If anything in this world can make a person happy, Xerxes should have been a very happy man.

Even as Xerxes held his feast in Susa, other kinds of feasts were taking place in Jerusalem. The Jews who had returned to Jerusalem reinstituted weekly and special yearly sacrifices in their rebuilt temple. Each one of those feasts pointed to the nature of God and to communication with Him as Lord and Creator. In Jerusalem, worshipers feasted on an animal after offering it as a sacrifice to God. We bow before each meal to remind ourselves that every meal should point us to God. We thank Him for the food He has provided.

Think of the contrast between Xerxes' banquets and the feasts Christ provided. When He yearned over the five thousand on that hillside above Galilee, He wanted to feed them. Certainly, He could have provided gold dishes. He could have brought on rich and exotic foods. Instead, He fed the multitude with what was available in a little boy's lunch: barley loaves, the food of the poor; and a local fish, something like sardines.

A girl who grew up in Korea said her family couldn't afford to buy the white rice that rich people bought. They had to eat brown rice. "Little did I know," she said, "how much better for me was the brown rice with all its vitamins intact." Little do most of us know how much better for us are the simple things God provides for us.

Yet Christ attended more elaborate feasts on occasion. He seemed to hallow them by His presence. Nothing is wrong with attending feasts as long as you go in the spirit of Christ.

Christ commanded us to remember Him by a ceremonial feast. He said the bread represented His body, bro-

ken for us; the wine His blood, shed for us (1 Cor.
11:23-25; Matt. 26). We all want to share in this feast
with Christ. We do, as we observe the Lord's Supper.
We also want to share in that glorious feast yet ahead,
"Blessed are those who are invited to the wedding banquet of the Lamb" (Rev. 19:9, BERK). Who will be
called? Anyone who puts his trust in Christ.

The theme of feasting and fasting runs through the
Book of Esther. Eating looms as an important activity in
everyone's life. We must choose how we will eat at life's
table. We can feast in a way that deprives others. Or we
can consume only enough to satisfy needs, then share
generously. The writer of Proverbs prayed,

Give me neither poverty nor riches,
Feed me with the food that is my portion,
Lest I be full and deny Thee and say,
"Who is the Lord?"
Or lest I be in want and steal,
And profane the name of my God (30:8-9, NASB).

Xerxes' banquets ended. How can the sense of feasting at life's table be made to last? "But the cheerful heart
has a continual feast" (Prov. 15:15, NIV). Your enjoyment of life doesn't depend upon the wealth of things
you're provided with. It depends upon the state of your
heart. If it's in right relationship with God, a sense of
feasting goes on throughout this life and into eternity.

2
Should a Wife Always Obey?

Any number of husbands ask their wives to grace occasions for them—sales meetings, weddings, dinners with clients, installations of officers, political rallies, class reunions. They're expected to smile, to allow themselves to be seen, but not obtrude as individuals in any way.

Occasionally, a husband graces an occasion for his wife. I recently saw two husbands sit through the installations of their wives as officers of a denominational organization for women. The only men present, they smiled and stood when introduced and then sat down.

Is it fair to ask another human being to give up precious hours of his lifetime to enrich an occasion for you? Some enjoy it; others don't. Political wives who rebel have been making headlines. They want to live their own lives, even to the extent of divorcing their husbands.

A young wife once told me her husband wanted her to accompany him to his college reunion. She said, "I don't know any of those people; I don't really care about going."

"He's proud of you. He wants to show you off," I said to her. She arranged for someone to take care of the children, and went.

To what extent does marital obligation give one or the other a claim in such situations? Ahasuerus and Vashti clashed over this very matter in the year 483 B.C. Both were hosting banquets. He sent for her to appear at his side. He wanted to show her off to a company of his leading men. She said no.

Why is space devoted in the Bible to a domestic conflict so long ago? Because it ended in Ahasuerus setting Vashti aside as a queen, and cleared the way for Esther, a Jewess. When an edict of the king would later threaten the Jews, Esther would be in a position to appeal to Ahasuerus for her people.

"Queen Vashti gave a banquet, too, for the women of King Ahasuerus' royal palace" (1:9, BERK).

Vashti's feast took place inside the palace, while the king entertained his guests in the garden. Perhaps space for all those people determined the arrangement.

Who was Vashti? The word means, in ancient Persian, the "desired one, the beloved," or the "beautiful woman."

Kings of Persia had to choose their legal wives from seven noble families. A cruel and vindictive woman, Amestris, appears in secular history as Xerxes' official wife. In so limited a choice, the king wouldn't likely find a ravishing beauty. Amestris was old enough that two of her sons accompanied Xerxes on his Greek campaign. One son married upon his return.

So probably Vashti was not the official queen, but the reigning favorite and queen of the harem. All oriental potentates possessed harems. Collecting beautiful women constituted a status symbol of the day. Solomon aped the surrounding kings with his 700 wives and 300 concubines. The custom persists all the way to the harems of some sheikhs in our century. That doesn't make the arrangements right, of course. God makes clear where Solomon's harem landed him (1 Kings 11:1-11).

"On the seventh day, when the heart of the king was merry with wine, he commanded Mehuman, Biztha, Harbona, Bigtha, Abagtha, Zethar, and Carkas, the seven eunuchs who served in the presence of King Ahasuerus, to bring Queen Vashti before the king with her royal crown in order to display her beauty to the people and the princes, for she was beautiful" (1:10-11, NASB).

A command—a formal request, sent by the king from his public banquet to the queen at her public banquet, and conveyed by seven eunuchs. Eunuchs had charge of the king's harem and also played an important role in administration of the empire.

King Ahasuerus didn't send a quiet message by one obscure servant, asking if his wife could please come and meet his guests. A modern husband may phone his wife and say, "Can you meet me at such and such a restaurant? I have some important clients." "Can you get over here to the reception? I'll wait for you." "Can you get to the rally?" A modern wife will usually try. A modern husband will usually take no for an answer if she's exhausted, if she can't get a baby-sitter, or if she's already entertaining some friends for luncheon.

But Ahasuerus didn't send any request. He boasted to his drinking party that the Beautiful One was coming. He'd already shown off all his riches and resources. Now he wanted to display his choicest possession for their envy—a living diamond. The king never dreamed she would refuse. Or maybe he did, and that's why he sent seven chamberlains, in the full panoply of a formal summons.

"But Queen Vashti refused to come when the king sent the eunuchs to tell her" (1:12, BECK).

The Bible doesn't tell us why Vashti wouldn't come. On searching, we find evidence that women commonly banqueted with men in ancient Persia. Esther invited Haman—a man—to banquet with the king and herself (5:8, 7:1). Nehemiah—a man—sat at table with both the king and queen in Susa (Neh. 2:6). Herodotus, a Greek historian contemporary with Xerxes, tells about some Persians who were entertained at a banquet in Greece. They asked for women at the banquet. Said the Persians, "Dear Macedonian, we Persians have a custom when we make a great feast to bring with us to the board our wives and concubines, and make them sit beside us."

Answered their Greek host, "O Persians! we have no such custom as this; but with us men and women are kept apart. Nevertheless . . . "

The Greeks brought in women, and the Persians insisted they sit at their sides. Then, the historian notes, "The Persians, who had drunk more than they ought, began to put their hands on them, and one even tried to give the woman next to him a kiss" (Herodotus 9.108-112).

So we can't say that Vashti refused because women didn't attend feasts with men in Persia. They did.

Maybe the wine made her feel quarrelsome. No doubt they drank at her banquet too. Certainly, alcohol can rob people of judgment. It often makes them quarrelsome and obstinate. "Wine is a scorner, strong drink a brawler, and whoever gets drunk is not wise'' (Prov. 20:1, BERK).

What a commotion Vashti stirred up!

"The king got very angry and his fury burned within him" (1:12, BECK).

The king had called all the great assemblage together to exhibit his power and authority. And he couldn't even command his wife!

Maybe the king's anger was partly at himself. Why had he set himself up for such a public humiliation? "It is not for kings to drink wine, nor for rulers to desire strong drink; lest they drink and forget what is decreed and pervert the rights of all the afflicted" (Prov. 31:4-5, BERK). Said a modern young man, "I don't drink because I don't want to give up command of myself at all times." He wanted to rule responsibly over the kingdom of his own life.

When the king recovered, he might well have wondered if the issue was worth losing his queen As a Christian, you learn how to take resistance to your will. It becomes a step in your training. Ahasuerus had never learned that fundamental lesson. Everything and everyone had to bend to his desires. He made Vashti's refusal a crisis of state and thereby separated himself from a valued queen.

When the queen recovered, she might have wondered if the issue was worth losing her position. True, Persian men behaved disgustingly at those drinking bouts. But they couldn't have put a hand on her in the king's presence. Any man would know such a move could mean instant death.

Vashti might also have wondered, at her leisure, if a softer answer could have turned away the king's wrath.

Any husband, wife, or parent knows the effect of a flat refusal, but may consider an appeal.

All these circumstances constituted part of God's plan. He created all the personalities involved—Ahasuerus, the advisors, and Vashti. Each acted freely according to his own personality. God blends the personalities and their behavior together, according to His master plan.

"Then the king spoke to the wise men who knew the times—you see, the king used to lay his matters before all who knew laws and religion . . . ." (1:13, BECK).

Ahasuerus showed some sense at this juncture—he asked advice. "Where there is no leadership, the people fall, but in an abundance of counselors there is safety" (Prov. 11:14, BERK). Angry, stirred by a wild impulse, half-drunk, certainly the king couldn't think straight. There's a time to ask advice, and a time to give good advice. Wise counselors might have urged him to consider how he had provoked the queen. Any person who wants obedience ought to consider carefully before he commands. He should leave the way open for face-saving retreat on some issues. "Would you like to . . . ?" "Do you mind . . . ?" "Would it be possible . . . ?"

But not Ahasuerus. He had charged out for conquest. His counselors, to keep their positions, had to support him. He couldn't retreat without losing face before all those guests.

Wise men, literally, "men of wisdom," show up often in Scripture. They included men who studied the stars, as well as those who studied laws and customs of past or current usage. Those consulted by Ahasuerus included heads of the seven noblest families of Persia.

These seven alone could approach the king without announcement at any time, except when he was in the company of one of his wives or concubines. (Compare Dan. 2:27, 5:15, Isa. 44:25, 47:13; Jer. 50:35; Ezra 7:14.)

"And the next unto him was Carshena, Shethar, Admatha, Tarshish, Meres, Marsena, and Memucan, the seven princes of Persia and Media, which saw the king's face, and which sat the first in the kingdom" (1:14).

Seven eunuchs in verse 10, and now seven princes; seven was a number sacred to Persians as well as to Hebrews. Keeping distant from his subjects constituted part of the king's mystique. Such distance also contributed to his safety.

King Ahasuerus put the big question to these counselors. But notice how he referred to Vashti:

" 'According to the law, what must be done to Queen Vashti because she didn't do what the king sent the eunuchs to tell her?'" (1:15, BECK)

Ahasuerus calls her *"Queen* Vashti." Did he want the counselors to provide a compromise whereby he might save face by severely punishing her? They did provide a compromise. She wasn't put to death; she was put out of the way. The king knew how to punish Vashti's refusal to obey him, but he didn't know how to gain her obedience to his wishes.

Counselors to a king, or leader, too often tell him what he wants to hear. The counselors have their own interests to look after. Perhaps these seven were already jealous of Vashti's power over Ahasuerus. They were only too happy to remove her influence.

What kind of advice do you give, when asked? Before you even start to give advice, you need to remove yourself from the picture. Look at the situation strictly from the point of view of the other's best interests. Only then can you think clearly, or see God's view of the matter.

"And Memucan answered before the king and the princes, 'Vashti the queen hath not done wrong to the king only, but also to all the princes, and to all the people that are in the provinces of the King Ahasuerus'" (1:16).

The power of example! The queen declined to come at the king's bidding, and so the dignified counselors pronounced that the whole kingdom would suffer. Women would, they predicted, get out of hand. The counselors proceeded to play on Ahasuerus' weaknesses like skilled performers on an instrument. They encouraged his whims and flattered his lowest instincts. Their objective was to gain their own ends.

"For this deed of the queen shall come abroad unto all women, so that they shall despise their husbands in their eyes, when it shall be reported, the King Ahasuerus commanded Vashti the queen to be brought in before him, but she came not" (1:17).

Vashti chose a most public occasion to humiliate her husband. We may wonder to what extent wives owe their husbands obedience. God's original plan for marriage is stated in Genesis: "Therefore shall a man leave his father and his mother, and shall cleave unto his wife: and they shall be one flesh" (2:24). That sounds pretty equal, with no problem in agreeing. They're one, each seeking to please the other. They identify totally.

Then sin entered the world. Man chose his own way. Adam and Eve wanted to go their own way, regardless of God and regardless of the effect on each other. God said the man would have to work hard for a living. To the woman He said, "Thy desire shall be to thy husband, and he shall rule over thee" (Gen. 3:16). Now she's limited too.

Once selfishness has entered, any corporation needs a head. It's a simple statement of fact that the man usually holds the upper hand. Who reads most of the books on marriage? Women. Who, usually, works hardest to keep a marriage together? The woman. Why? Because once a man has claimed her physically, her desire is for him. If she robs him of a sense of dominance over her, he can't even perform physically. Is it fair? Who can say? It's the way it is.

So the Bible goes on to tell how the sexes can live in good relationship in a sinful world. God has constituted man as the head, with all attendant responsibilities. When a wife robs her husband of his headship, she also excuses him from his responsibilities. He feels the release and acts accordingly. Throughout Scripture, throughout history, many have lived below the highest ideal of marriage.

In the Christian pattern of marriage, we go back to the original ideal: "Submitting yourselves one to another in the fear of God. Wives, submit yourselves to your own husbands, as unto the Lord" (Eph. 5:21-22). Do all you can to please him. You don't have to submit to all men in the same way. Don't get married if you don't want to give a man the headship. Such a concept of marriage will work out to a woman's best interests in the end.

God places a limitation on husbands. They're not granted a right to rule by whim as did Ahasuerus. "Husbands, love your wives, even as Christ also loved the church and gave Himself for it" (Eph. 5:25, see also Eph. 5:21-33).

Certainly, the king's command showed lack of respect to Vashti as a person. He didn't consult her wishes. He didn't consider that she might feel responsibility to stay at the banquet of the women. He didn't consider that she might not feel honored to appear as the only woman before an assembly of drunken men. Maybe she felt belittled that he wanted to display her as a prize piece of flesh, like a thoroughbred horse or pedigree dog.

As a parent, husband, or wife, you know which requests or commands will stir unreasonable opposition. A helpful rule to follow with children is to give as few commands as possible, and see that those few are enforced. A husband wanting to secure the respect of his household will use a direct command only as a last resort. He'll depend on loving respect from his wife and children to secure headship in his family. A wife will find it easy to obey the wishes of such a husband even before he speaks them. He shouldn't need to command. An ideal marriage is not built on law. It is built on love.

"This very day the princesses of Persia and Media who learn of the queen's behavior will so respond to all the king's princes, and there will be plenty of contempt and bad temper" (1:18, BERK).

Your conduct influences that of other people. What constitutes your sphere of influence? How many people are likely to follow your example? Jesus pronounced woe on those who create stumbling blocks for others (Matt. 18:7).

"If it pleases the king, let him make a royal declaration, and let it be written among the laws of the Persians and

Medes and never changed, that Vashti should no more come before King Xerxes; and let the king make another, a better woman, his queen" (1:19 BECK).

Now we know the background for the story of Esther, and how there came to be a vacancy in the queenship. We've also been introduced to the power and splendor of the king and we know Esther's position to be none too secure. A man who'd set aside one favorite would also set aside another.

"And when the king's decree which he shall make shall be published throughout all his empire, (for it is great,) all the wives shall give to their husbands honor, both to great and small" (1:20).

Those governors and princes gained official sanction for selfishness. The decree would inspire all wives to fear their husbands. It would also make all husbands tyrants. What a far cry from the give and take of marriage that the Bible shows us in so many Hebrew homes! What a contrast to the tender love God intended between the sexes!

"And the saying pleased the king and the princes; and the king did according to the word of Memucan" (1:21).

The king's action ends the story of Vashti so far as the Book of Esther is concerned. Though once the reigning favorite, Vashti disappears from the record. She may have perished, or she joined the other wives and concubines whom the king never called for.

"For he sent letters into all the king's provinces, into every province according to the writing thereof, and to

every people after their language, that every man should
bear rule in his own house, and that it should be pub-
lished according to the language of every people''
(1:22).

Here we're introduced to the remarkable postal system of
the Persian empire. It will figure in the story later.

We know from inscriptions found at Persepolis and
Susa that Persian kings sent out proclamations in more
than one language.

We also learn that each man could hereby speak his
native tongue in his own household. The empire encom-
passed people of many languages. Each wife was to
speak her husband's mother tongue.

Why was such an edict needed? Was a women's liber-
ation movement stirring? Were women in the Persian
empire trying to kick off some shackles? Could this edict
reaching into the home really be enforced? Or was the
whole thing only a court intrigue to get rid of a strong-
minded queen? The Bible doesn't tell us. We really don't
need to know.

What the Book of Esther does tell us is that God works
in mysterious ways His wonders to perform. He works
through people motivated by passion, ambition, and selfishness, as well as by noble motives.

God is going to rescue the whole Jewish nation from
destruction without a single supernatural act—no miraculous interventions in the Book of Esther. Yet the whole
book builds up to a total miracle, detail by detail. God
stands in the shadows, keeping watch over His own,
whether or not anybody recognizes His hand arranging
circumstances.

3
A
Special
Bond

God has a way of showing us that everything this world affords proves to be flawed.

"This house brought me to the Lord," a young man said as he ushered us into his living room.

"How's that?" We asked, knowing that losses often bring people to the Lord, but luxurious houses and grounds such as this too often distract from spiritual things. We'd known the young couple years before to be very careless church members. Now my husband, Bart, was speaking at their church and they had asked to entertain us.

"You remember when you used to call me up, trying to get me to come to church? Well, then I thought, 'I don't need the church; I'm too busy building my business. Getting everything I want will satisfy me.'

"When we moved into this house, I realized I had acquired everything I ever dreamed of. And I wasn't happy. I still had to cope with endless problems. A beautiful oak tree died; the foundation shifted; the roof leaked. There was always something. The house just didn't satisfy me the way I thought it would.

"I knew then I needed the Lord. Now I work for Him. And our whole family life has changed."

The Book of Esther gives a picture of life in the highest places the world can offer. Millions viewed Ahasuerus and those who walked his courts as floating in paradise with no problems, while ordinary people had to grub for a living at menial tasks.

Americans tend to feel that to find happiness they must acquire a new car, a bigger house, a better-paying job. The old car, house, and job haven't brought the satisfaction they want, but *more* might.

The Book of Esther shows how really miserable people can be, even in the highest places. It also shows opportunities for good in privileged positions.

"After these things . . . " (2:1)

"After these things" could mean anytime from two hours to two years. We know that Xerxes spent two more years in preparations after assembling his leading men. Then he left to invade Greece. The conversation about finding a successor to Vashti (vv. 2-4) must have taken place before he left. In two more years (2:16) Esther would be chosen queen. When chosen, she would have spent a year in the harem preparing to meet the king. It would certainly have taken the other year for officials to gather maidens from the Empire.

"When the wrath of King Ahasuerus was appeased, he remembered Vashti, and what she had done and what was decreed against her" (2:1).

Ahasuerus, amid all his wealth and splendor, felt an oppressive want. He remembered the beauty, charm, and loveliness of Vashti. Now she was gone. The author subtly suggests the king wanted to reinstate Vashti. But he couldn't because of his irrevocable decree.

Many would envy Ahasuerus' freedom to do whatever he pleased. No one dared oppose him. But, free to rule by whim, he became a slave to himself. No one restrained him in his fit of anger. Now he grieved for a lost queen. What foolish mistakes have loved ones and friends kept you from making?

Likewise, millions of women from Africa to India must have envied Vashti. They thought of her living in dreamy indolence as they ground grain with heavy millstones, carried water, spun yarn, baked bread at primitive ovens, and carried infants on their backs.

But when you have satisfied all your physical wants, you have time to think about your feelings of dissatisfaction and longing.

Vashti's feelings must have tortured her. She now had no true relationship with the king and lacked the security of her position. She was doomed to spend the rest of her life in luxurious confinement and unutterable boredom.

"Then the king's attendants, who served him, said, 'Let beautiful young virgins be sought for the king. And let the king appoint overseers in all the provinces of his kingdom that they may gather every beautiful young virgin to Susa the capital, to the harem, into the custody of Hegai, the king's eunuch, who was in charge of the women; and let their cosmetics be given them. Then let the young lady who pleases the king be queen in place of Vashti'" (2:2-4, NASB).

The attendants became alarmed. Would the king take out on them his regret for Vashti? They must think up something to distract his mind.

The king never had to face himself and his own weaknesses, for people stood by to play up to his appetites. We do children a disservice if we don't let them reap the results of their own acts. If a child who spends his weekly allowance in two days can go to Grandma for more, he'll never learn to handle money.

If father comes to the rescue every time Sonny gets into an accident, he'll never learn to drive safely. One night at 3:00 A.M. ,we heard a terrible crash. A car had slammed head-on into one parked in front of our house. A drunken youth slumped over the wheel, unharmed. Police summoned his father who appeared on the scene and took him home. It took three weeks for the owner of the parked car to collect insurance and replace her own car. By that time the boy's father had already bought him a new car. His insurance company said it was the eighth accident for the boy. Father paid the exorbitant insurance premiums.

Ahasuerus imagined that he ruled, but he didn't. Actually, those about him tossed him back and forth like a Ping-Pong ball, trying to score for themselves.

Those attendants wanted to win favor from the king. They also wanted to distract him from any thought of bringing Vashti back. Women of the harem often took part in palace intrigues. Imagine Vashti's retaliation on any who took part in her demotion! All sought to manipulate the king.

A true friend doesn't manipulate. He tells you what you ought to hear. "Faithful are the wounds of a friend" (Prov. 27:6). "He that rebuketh a man afterwards shall find more favor than he that flattereth with the tongue" (Prov. 28:23).

"The suggestion appealed to the king and he acted accordingly" (2:4, BERK).

Ahasuerus didn't concern himself with how he wronged
those women he locked up for life. He deprived probably
three or four hundred of a normal life, of husbands who
could concentrate on them alone. He didn't think of the
men he wronged. Just one of those beautiful girls might
have made an ordinary man happy.

The king did only what pleased himself. God asks us
to think about pleasing each other, "Therefore all things
whatsoever you would that men should do to you, do you
even so to them" (Matt. 7:12).

Yet God was at work through all those selfish maneu-
verings.

"Now there was in the citadel of Susa a Jew" (2:5, NIV).

A Jew? In Susa the capital? But hadn't Cyrus given the
Jews permission to go back to Jerusalem? Of course.
Some 50 years before, in 536 B.C. (Ezra 1:2-4). Some
did go back, under Zerubbabel. Another group would yet
return under Ezra.

But other Jews found conditions comfortable in Persia, Babylonia, and Assyria. They became successful in
business, in government, and in the crafts. They liked
the land of their adoption—for many, the land of their
birth—as Jews have throughout history. The pioneer life
of rebuilding Jerusalem didn't appeal to them.

Yet the Jews persisted as a distinct nation. The Book
of Esther shows God caring for His people outside the
Land, as He has throughout history, whether faithful to
Him or not.

Should Mordecai have gone back? We don't know.
Maybe he wanted to but couldn't. God used him where
he was.

A young woman wanted to go abroad as a foreign
missionary, but family circumstances prevented her. She

devoted a lifetime to mission work in this country: to blacks in the inner city, to neighbors, and to service in her church.

"Whose name was Mordecai" (2:5).

The name means "belonging to Marduk," patron deity of Babylon. Strange name for a Jew! But perhaps it had lost its original meaning and had become just a name in Persian society.

Mordecai lived in the palace or capital, the fortified part of the city on the acropolis above the town. So he must have been connected with the royal service. Ordinary folk lived across the river in the town.

"The son of Jair, the son of Shimei, the son of Kish, a Benjamite; who had been carried away from Jerusalem with the captivity which had been carried away with Jeconiah, king of Judah, whom Nebuchadnezzar the king of Babylon had carried away" (2:5-6).

Mordecai and Esther came from noble forebears and a strong Hebrew background. When Nebuchadnezzar carried Judah away into captivity, he took the cream of the population (2 Kings 25). So Mordecai's great-grandfather Kish, carried away at that time, must have been a man of some distinction.

Mordecai and his cousin Esther came from the tribe of Benjamin—always closely associated with the royal tribe of Judah. Saul, the first king, was a Benjamite (1 Sam. 9:21). His father's name was Kish too, a name that became common especially in the tribe of Benjamin. These two tribes of Judah and Benjamin remained faithful to Jehovah long after the 10 tribes were carried into captivity.

"And he brought up Hadassah, that is, Esther, his uncle's daughter: for she had neither father nor mother, and the maid was fair and beautiful; whom Mordecai, when her father and mother were dead, took for his own daughter" (2:7).

If a cousin of yours became orphaned, would you assume responsibility for the child? Mordecai did. Bringing up a child involves time, money, space in your house, griefs, joys, and responsibilities. All this Mordecai took upon himself when his father's brother died and little Hadassah needed a guardian.

A modern couple in their 30s adopted two children, a brother and sister aged five and seven. The children had lived in various foster homes. The adoptive mother said, "Many people are willing to adopt infants. We wanted to take some children who might not find a home otherwise."

Mordecai saw a need. He voluntarily filled it and brought upon himself many blessings. "He that hath a bountiful eye shall be blessed; for he giveth of his bread to the poor" (Prov. 22:9).

Like many other great characters of history, Esther first appears as a humble figure, a helpless waif. Her Hebrew name, Hadassah, meant myrtle. Esther is a name derived from the Assyrian "Ishtar," the goddess of youth and beauty.

Mordecai comes on stage as a principal character of the story. He fills the most active role, and in many ways becomes the most important character of all. Watch for all the ways in which he affects the actions of others. When we look at the Book of Esther as a microcosm of Jewish history and persecution, we see Mordecai as symbolic of the Jew. He is always referred to as "the Jew."

As a Jew, Mordecai brought up little Hadassah in the

learning and tradition of his ancestors. Like any Jewish parent, he would teach her the Scriptures, instruct her about the holy days, and observe the various ceremonies of the home, including the Passover feast with its roast lamb and bitter herbs. All were observances which would become dear to her. Mordecai himself was strongly steeped in Jewish tradition.

Whatever Mordecai taught Esther, he certainly imbued her with patriotism for Israel. You teach patriotism by teaching history. Esther must have learned the tales of past heroes. Though surrounded with all the temptations of a heathen court, Mordecai never forgot his roots. Neither did Esther.

What are your roots? Your roots form part of your identity. Perhaps you can trace certain qualities of industry, thrift, faith, or opposite qualities to your ancestry. When should you remain faithful to your roots? When should you cut free from your roots and graft yourself onto another tree?

A postman's wife wanted to adopt a baby girl. Her husband only half-willingly assented. In a few years the woman died. The child felt unloved and unwanted. But she belonged to the Lord. Church women filled in for her dead mother. When she grew up she married and had a child. She also adopted herself into another family by generous and loving help with their children. When those children grew up they always thought of her as "aunt." They visited back and forth with her. She became family to them.

Esther and many others could echo the broader meaning of this verse, "When my father and my mother forsake me, then the Lord will take me up" (Ps. 27:10).

"So it came to pass, when the king's commandment and his decree was heard and when many maidens were

gathered together unto Shushan the palace, to the custody of Hegai, that Esther was brought also unto the king's house, to the custody of Hegai, keeper of the women" (2:8).

Did Mordecai bring Esther voluntarily to join a pagan king's harem? Jewish law expressly forbade intermarriage with Gentiles. Did Mordecai have no choice? Or did ambition prompt him to present her? Did Esther feel compelled by Mordecai's sense of responsibility for his race? The Bible doesn't tell us.

We can picture throughout the empire ambitious parents, government officials, and local bigwigs putting forward the most beautiful girls of their regions. Each family, tribe, or province would hope to leap suddenly into prominence through a single, lovely maiden. We can also picture the homesickness and terror as those girls faced brutal competition for the king's favor.

Esther, along with scores of others, entered the women's quarters of the palace. These have been identified in the ruins at Susa. She left the tender nurture of Mordecai for the custody of Hegai. How would she fare?

"The girl pleased him and won his favor. Immediately he provided her with her beauty treatments and special food. He assigned to her seven maids selected from the king's palace and moved her and her maids into the best place in the harem" (2:9, NIV).

The mystery of special favor—why did Hegai favor Esther over the others? Who can define beauty in a girl? It comes in so many different styles. Yet something about Esther made her stand out. The qualification for competing suggested nothing except physical attributes. Certainly God had equipped Esther with unusual beauty. In addition, Mordecai as a true Jew taught her to value inward qualities more than the outward. "Man looketh on the outward appearance, but the Lord looketh on the heart" (1 Sam. 16:7).

Hegai knew the king's taste. He immediately saw Esther as the probable successor to Vashti. Perhaps a certain poise, a certain independence of mind marked her as different. Politicians try to get on the bandwagon early by picking out the winner. Likewise, Hegai hoped to gain favor for himself in the future by favoring Esther.

"Esther did not make known her people or her kindred, for Mordecai had instructed her that she should not make them known" (2:10, NASB).

How could Esther observe Jewish dietary laws and keep the Sabbath in the harem without revealing her Jewishness? Some say she couldn't and that she must have ignored these laws. Before Hitler's persecution of Jews in Germany, many Jews had become totally identified with German society. They thought they had lost their identity as Jews.

But a Jewish commentator on Esther suggests how she managed to keep the Sabbath in the harem. She simply assigned her seven maidens one to each day. Thus none would know that she observed the Sabbath day differently from other days. He says she could have observed Jewish dietary laws as a vegetarian eating only natural foods in their uncooked state. Thereby she could avoid non-kosher food.

To the Jews, Esther stands out as a great heroine. They call their women's Zionist organization in the United States "Hadassah." The women of this largest Jewish organization in the world support the Hadassah Hospital in Jerusalem.

Why did Mordecai charge Esther not to show her nationality? Was he afraid the name "Jew" would bring discrimination against her? Did he want to protect her from unpleasantness? Did his ambition for her motivate him? Or ambition for himself? If his motives weren't mixed, he wouldn't have been human.

We see here the close bond between Esther and Mordecai. A child taught when little to love and respect his parents carries the same attitudes into adulthood. Mordecai held no outward control over Esther once she entered the palace. But he had built a strong relationship with her when God gave him the opportunity. You can't overestimate the importance of the time you spend, the effort you make, in the early years of a child's life. As the story progresses, we'll see how God worked through a daughter's habit of obedience.

"And Mordecai walked every day before the court of the women's house, to know how Esther did, and what should become of her" (2:11).

Mordecai showed intense concern for his ward. Only authorized eunuchs could enter the harem, but Mordecai could find out about Esther through them. It took some effort to keep in communication with her. But he made that effort. He had invested a lot of himself in her.

If you are a parent of grown children, you watch over them, keep in touch with them, and pray for them, though you have no direct control over them. Whatever bonds you built or didn't build with your children in the past affect your relationship today. Some mistakes you can overcome. Some you have to turn over to the Lord to remedy. "Train up a child in the way he should go: and when he is *old* he will not depart from it" (Prov. 22:6). If you put in the training, you can depend upon that promise when the child grows old. He may go through some trying stages in the meantime.

Paul wrote, "Children, obey your parents in the Lord" (Eph. 6:1). Grown children must make their own decisions. But the Bible says to everyone, "Honor thy father and thy mother: that thy days may be long" (Ex. 20:12). You can always listen with respect to a parent's advice. Quite often it proves good. Esther listened and heeded.

At this time Xerxes must have been away from the palace, carrying on his campaign in Greece, while officials gathered the beauties and Esther was putting in her year of preparation. The author of Esther concerns himself with the fate of Jews in the Persian empire; and with the harem as it will affect the fate of the Jews.

Herodotus, the Greek historian, interests himself in Persia only as its history affects Greece. He records only sketchy notes on Xerxes' domestic life, nothing about his harem. He does record several affairs Xerxes carried on with other men's wives. These suggest Xerxes plunged into sensuality to drown his humiliation at the hands of the Greeks. The Book of Esther gives us a segment of history we would otherwise know nothing about.

"Now when every maid's turn was come to go in to King Ahasuerus, after that she had been twelve months, according to the manner of the women—for so were the days of their purifications accomplished, to wit, six months with oil of myrrh, and six months with sweet odors, and with other things for the purifying of the women . . . ." (2:12)

Twelve months in quarantine were required before a maiden could approach the pampered king—perhaps to make sure she carried no diseases, suffered no irregularities. Twelve months to train her in the use of costly perfumes and creams. Voluptuousness turned into an art and a toil. No inward preparation whatever is suggested and no education or training for high office.

How did Esther spend this time? We don't know. Jewish commentators like to think she read the Scriptures, prayed to her God, and kept faithful.

In such an atmosphere of luxurious ease, girls would be tempted to forget all obligations and have no thoughts except to please the king and secure comforts for themselves. We can marvel that Esther arose as a strong and unselfish woman. She overcame insuperable temptations. Did her respect for Mordecai as parent help Esther keep her perspective?

How would you spend such a period of confinement? What would you do to maintain perspective?

"And this is how she would go to the king: Anything she wanted was given to her to take with her from the harem to the king's palace" (2:13, NIV).

Imagine yourself turned loose in a modern department store with an unlimited charge account. What would you select to make yourself attractive for some special occasion?

Imagine how overdone some of the girls must have looked. Decked out in too much clothing and jewelry; hairdos far too fancy. They must have cloyed the king as he sampled one girl after another, each as physically beautiful as the last.

"In the evening she went, and on the morrow she returned into the second house of the women, to the custody of Shaashgaz, the king's chamberlain, which kept the concubines. She came in unto the king no more, ex-

cept the king delighted in her, and that she were called by name" (2:14).

In this beauty contest a girl didn't go her own way if she lost out to someone else. Instead she moved into the house of the concubines, those who had spent at least one night with the king. Of these, few ever visited him again, and then only if called by name. The rest lived out their days locked up in the women's quarters.

"Now when the turn of Esther, the daughter of Abihail the uncle of Mordecai, who had taken her for his daughter, was come to go in unto the king, she required nothing but what Hegai, the king's chamberlain, the keeper of the women, appointed. And Esther obtained favor in the sight of all them that looked upon her" (2:15).

Maybe Esther wasn't very anxious to please the king. Perhaps she really didn't care to win the contest. Or perhaps she showed her shrewdness, or her confidence in her unadorned beauty.

Or maybe Esther carried over the habit of obedience she had learned from Mordecai. Now it served her in good stead. She submitted her judgment to that of Hegai. As an experienced keeper of the harem, he knew what pleased the king. He understood the simplicity of dress that would make Esther stand out from the others.

Esther's modesty on this occasion won the favor of everyone who saw her. Her simplicity of dress only served to set off her natural beauty of face and form.

The New Testament gives some good guidance about clothes: "Your adornment should not be outward—braided hair, putting on gold trinkets, or putting on robes; instead it should be the inner personality of the heart with the imperishable qualities of a gentle and quiet spirit, something of surpassing value in God's sight'' (1 Peter 3:3-4, BERK).

Clothes or jewelry should never suggest that you look to them for your sense of worth. You want your body to look its best as the temple of the Holy Spirit: healthy, well-exercised, properly fed, clean. In dress, you don't want to look cheap. In different societies, various articles of clothing and jewelry carry differing symbolic values. Respect the conventions of the society in which you live.

Bart and I were preparing for a three-month preaching and teaching mission to the Philippines. A Filipino girl studying in America looked me over. ''The length of your dress is all right. Don't wear dresses too short. And short sleeves are OK. But don't wear any sleeveless dresses. And little if any make-up. These things would mark you in the Philippines as a woman of questionable character.'' I respected her advice.

A Christian needs to take care not to send out false signals by what she wears.

''So Esther was taken unto King Ahasuerus into his house royal in the tenth month, which is the month Tebeth, in the seventh year of his reign'' (2:16).

Before the inscriptions identified Ahasuerus positively with Xerxes, critics questioned these dates. (Compare 1:3.) Why would Ahasuerus wait four years before filling Vashti's place? The gap seemed to them unlikely. But it proves historically essential to account for Xerxes' Greek campaign.

The king must have felt sated with people who fawned over him. Perhaps Esther's dignity appealed to him. He had tasted all the world offered. Perhaps Esther suggested a hint of something different and higher.

A sense of relationship to God can give you a sense of self-worth. You can feel free before men. You don't have to clutch for their favor. A person who doesn't clutch at others seems all the more desirable.

Esther did not depend upon her beauty, nor upon Ahasuerus. She apparently put her trust in God, even in that situation. If God wanted her to win, she would win. If He wanted her to pass unnoticed, she would pass unnoticed. Your relationship to God proves of greater importance than your relationship to any human being. God loves you. Knowing that enables you to respect and love yourself. A sense of God's love can give you dignity and self-respect in any situation.

"And the king loved Esther above all the women, and she obtained grace and favor in his sight more than all the virgins; so that he set the royal crown upon her head, and made her queen instead of Vashti. Then the king made a great feast unto all his princes and his servants, even Esther's feast; and he made a release to the provinces, and gave gifts, according to the state of the king" (2:17-18).

Again, a great feast. Ahasuerus wanted to celebrate his selection of Esther as queen. As we do, Persians celebrated great events and honored special persons with feasts. In addition, Ahasuerus proclaimed a holiday throughout the empire. Of course, he gave gifts worthy of a king. That's how monarchs kept their soldiers and sycophants around them.

God had his agents, Esther and Mordecai, in position. The danger to the Jews hadn't even arisen yet, but Isaiah reminds us, "Before they call, I will answer" (65:24).

How many times has God made ready the answer to your prayer before you even prayed it? God worked through a wife's disobedience to clear the way for Esther. He worked through a daughter's obedience to bring Esther to a place of influence.

4
Civic Duty and You

God has placed Jews in influential positions at various times in history.

"What kind of reward do you wish for your services?" the British government asked a man named Chaim Weizmann.

"Only one kind of reward: a national home in Palestine for my people, the Jews."

The year was 1917. Why did the most powerful empire on earth at that time feel so indebted to one Jew? Britain stood on the brink of defeat in World War I. No American divisions were yet prepared for the fighting. The British Minister of Ammunitions, Lloyd George, "happened" to mention to a friend the scarcity of a certain chemical, acetone. The British Navy couldn't carry on without it. The friend "happened" to know of a brilliant scientist who might solve the problem. Engaged for the task, the man experimented till he found a solution.

The brilliant scientist "happened" to be a Jew. This particular Jew, Chaim Weizmann, had already presented the cause of Zionism to British cabinet officials whenever he saw an opportunity. Working on the acetone problem brought him into increased contact with important officials. The British mandate to make Palestine a homeland for the Jewish people grew largely out of Weizmann's influence.

Intensely concerned about his people, Weizmann also labored as a loyal British subject. In like fashion, Mordecai, a faithful Jew, loyally served the Persian government. He too turned out to be in the right place at the right moment to speak for his people.

"Mordecai was sitting at the king's gate" (2:19, NIV).

To us, anyone sitting at a gate must be a gatekeeper or guard. But this was not so in the East. At the gate officials received petitioners and dealt with government business. There judges sat, and ordinary people came to get differences settled (Herodotus *History* 3.120).

Mordecai might have sat as some kind of judge or official for the king. An undated cuneiform text has been found which mentions a certain Mordecai (Marduka). He is referred to as a high official at the court of Susa during the reign of Xerxes even before the third year, when the Book of Esther opens.

What was the gate like? At Susa, archeologists found remains of a fortified gate, square and tower-like. Xerxes' summer palace at Persepolis has an elaborate gateway with sphinxes. If you pass through the double gate, you can still sit on the stone benches inside that were once used by Mordecai and his fellow courtiers.

Daniel also "sat in the gate" when he served as a member of the court of King Nebuchadnezzar of Babylon (Dan. 2:48-49).

"And when the virgins were gathered together the second time, then . . ." (2:19)

Why a second gathering of virgins? (There is no article, i.e. *the,* in the Hebrew.) The words must mean what they obviously say. A second bevy of beautiful girls appeared at the palace even after the king selected Esther.

No wonder Esther enjoyed no sense of security in the king's affections! (See 4:11.) How much happiness could she find in such a relationship, despite its giddy height? God gives ample evidence in Esther's story that man's laws for marriage don't produce happiness. God's law is that each woman should have her own husband (1 Cor. 7:2).

"Esther had not yet made known her kindred or her people, even as Mordecai had commanded her, for Esther did what Mordecai told her as she had done when under his care" (2:20, NASB).

Is there a time not to speak? Peter and Philippa (not their real names) moved into a suburb of Pittsburgh from another state. No one paid much attention to them except one family down the block whom they met through their children. Don and Jeanette invited them over and asked if they were interested in finding a church. They said no.

The couples continued as friends. After some months the two-year-old child of Peter and Philippa became seriously ill. Philippa haunted the hospital. Jeanette cared for their older child, sent in meals, and helped with housework.

One time Philippa asked Jeanette how she could do so much for comparative strangers in the community. Jeanette replied, ''Christ in my heart makes me want to do these things.''

They carried on long discussions during which Peter and Philippa expressed bitterness about the church. But Jeanette never gave up. Today, Peter and Philippa over flow with Christ and function as joyful church members. They say Don and Jeanette made the difference.

Should Jeanette immediately have told them of her relationship to Christ?

The preacher in Ecclesiastes, reasoning from a common sense point of view, said, "There is an appointed time for everything . . . . A time to be silent, and a time to speak" (3:1, 7, NASB).

Mordecai at first told Esther not to proclaim her Jewish ancestry. Persians considered only Persians their real equals. They accepted the Medes, living next to them, but people living farther away were thought to be inferior. Jews came from far away, and Persians viewed them with disdain as a subject nation.

Esther would have had to come from one of the seven noble Persian families to become the official queen. But as a harem favorite, she could stand or fall on her own charms. Mordecai told her not to point out what could only arouse prejudice. Later he would tell her the time had come to declare her identity.

"In those days, while Mordecai sat in the king's gate, two of the king's chamberlains, Bigthan and Teresh, of those which kept the door, were wroth, and sought to lay hands on the King Ahasuerus" (2:21).

Mordecai still occupied the same position at court as before Esther became queen. In the East, if a person rises in the world, his relatives expect to rise with him. The solidarity of the family unit gives all relatives a claim. But Mordecai asserted no claim.

He discharged his regular duties, kept his ears open, and his mind busy. He heard of a plan to kill the king. Two who guarded the door, perhaps the king's private room, plotted against him.

Despots lived with the constant threat of assassination. To their subjects, death was the only way to remove an absolute monarch. One after another of Israel's kings died at the hand of an assassin (1 Kings 15:27; 16:9-10; 2 Kings 9:14-24; 15:10, 25; 21:23). Also, kings of Damascus (2 Kings 8:15) and Assyria (2 Kings 19:37). Xerxes himself was assassinated in a similar plot 14 years later.

Xerxes never knew who around him might be plotting his death. Courtiers could find many reasons to become angry, such as favors given or favors withheld.

We all must learn to live with some uncertainty in life for ourselves and loved ones. Christ gives us our only real security. In Him we can face the risks of every day. Jesus said, "I am the Resurrection and the Life; he who believes in Me shall live even if he dies, and everyone who lives and believes in Me shall never die" (John 11:25-26, NASB). Ahasuerus knew no such assurance.

"But Mordecai heard of it and told Queen Esther, who in his name informed the king" (2:22, BERK).

People didn't know of Mordecai's relationship to Esther. Perhaps the plotters asked Mordecai to take part; perhaps he overheard rumors and traced them down. Had Mordecai not learned of this plot, the chain of events would lack a necessary link. For Mordecai became God's instrument for delivering the Jews by gaining special favor with the king.

The Bible makes clear that God's people are to support the government under which they live. God allowed Mordecai to learn about the plot. Mordecai acted on the knowledge as a loyal subject in the employ of the king. Joseph, in Egypt, assisted those with whom his lot was cast. Daniel served the king of Babylon faithfully. Nehemiah, at Susa, held an honorable position next to the king. All, at the same time, remained faithful to God.

Jeremiah wrote, "Thus says the Lord. . . . Seek the welfare of the city where I have sent you into exile, and pray to the Lord for it; for its welfare shall be your welfare" (Jer. 29:4, 7, BERK).

The Bible teaches that Christians hold a double citizenship—in the country where they live, and in heaven. Jesus said, "Render therefore unto Caesar the things which are Caesar's; and unto God the things that are God's" (Matt. 22:21). Have you ever encountered any difficulty in drawing the line between those two loyalties? Do you know of anyone who has?

"And when inquisition was made of the matter, it was found out; therefore they were both hanged on a tree: and it was written in the Book of the Chronicles before the king" (2:23).

Have you ever performed some service for which you expected a reward or at least a thank you, and you received nothing? Ancient writers mention the record books the kings of Persia kept. Scribes wrote down acts of faithfulness, with a view to reward.

God's timing is seen here. Perhaps the king ordered a reward. It could have become lost in bureaucratic red tape. For five long years Mordecai's good deed lay interred in a closed book. Mordecai returned to his old job, content that he had done the right thing. Content to leave the matter of reward with God.

God doesn't overlook the slightest effort that honors Him. He has "a book of remembrance" (Mal. 3:16). Paul referred to "the Book of Life," where the names of those who shared his struggles in the Gospel are written (Phil. 4:3). God will call up your good deeds and good thoughts in His own timing, as he did for the faithful

Mordecai.

"After these things did King Ahasuerus promote Haman, the son of Hammedatha the Agagite, and advanced him, and set his seat above all the princes that were with him" (3:1).

Before danger arose, God put His agents, Mordecai and Esther, in place for the Jews' deliverance. But why did He allow that danger to arise? It must have been to bring His power to the attention of a careless people. They learned of their need of dependence upon Him.

Why does God allow storm, stress, catastrophe, and petty annoyance in our lives? So we won't forget to put our hands in His. How we relate to Him stands supremely important in life. We can rejoice in difficulties as they point us to Him.

We soon see Haman as a scoundrel, interested only in himself. To the Jews, Haman was an Agagite, a spiritual, if not physical, descendant of King Agag of the Amalekites, who were enemies of Israel. The Amalekites tried to stop Israel from entering the Promised Land (Ex. 17:8-16; Num. 14:45). God later ordered Saul to destroy them. He removed Saul from the kingship for not obeying completely (1 Sam. 15).

King Ahasuerus, absorbed in pleasure, didn't care to slave away at details of government. He handed over to Haman the day-to-day work of ruling.

"And all the king's servants, that were in the king's gate, bowed, and reverenced Haman: for the king had so commanded concerning him. But Mordecai bowed not, nor did him reverence" (3:2).

In the Orient, everybody prostrated himself before superiors. Why did the king have to issue special orders to bow down to Haman? Perhaps Haman's appointment stirred general opposition; many might have seen him as an evil man or as an upstart unqualified for high office. In Jewish lore, he represents the epitome of evil, as Judas does to Christians.

Why did Mordecai rile such a person by refusing him the customary gesture of respect? Mordecai supported Ahasuerus' government. Haman represented that government. Why did Mordecai make such an issue?

Peter wrote to the church, "Honor all men; love the brotherhood, fear God, honor the king" (1 Peter 2:17, NASB). Paul wrote, "Render therefore to all their dues . . . honor to whom honor." (See Rom. 13:1-8.)

The Bible doesn't say why Mordecai refused to prostrate himself. It simply tells how his refusal led to threat of extinction for the whole Jewish race.

"Then the king's servants, which were in the king's gate, said unto Mordecai, 'Why transgressest thou the king's commandment?'" (3:3)

"If I have to wash my hands before eating," says the child picking at his brother, "you do too. Mama, he didn't wash his hands." Likewise, none of us wants someone else to get by without paying his income tax.

Other employees serving at the gate didn't want Mordecai to get by without bowing down to Haman. They prostrated themselves, as ordered, however they felt about Haman. Mordecai stood stubbornly upright. Haman didn't notice at first. The other servants didn't report to Haman immediately. They watched Mordecai daily, reminding him of his duty. But Mordecai paid no attention. The only reason he gave for not bowing was that he was a Jew.

What difference should that make? Jews normally prostrated themselves before their own kings (see 1 Sam. 24:8; 2 Sam. 14:4; 1 Kings 1:16), as well as before other people on occasion (see Gen. 23:7, 27:29, 33:3.) Mordecai would certainly have to prostrate himself before the king when he succeeded Haman as prime minister (Herodotus 1.134; 3.86; 8.118).

Was Mordecai expressing his Jewish national spirit and pride in refusing allegiance to Haman? If Haman were really a descendant of the Amalekite King Agag, Mordecai would hate Haman with ancestral blood hatred. If he were only nicknamed "Agagite" because of his known enmity to the Jews, Mordecai would still hate him.

Should Mordecai have refused customary respect for the office Haman held? A delegation of Greeks refused to bow down before the Persian king. They considered it unmanly and said it was not a Greek custom (Herodotus 7.136). But it was Oriental custom, and Mordecai was an Oriental.

Opposing forces in Esther now stand arrayed. Evil will grow stronger. But God sits on His throne—far above Ahasuerus; far above Haman.

5

Is Your Prejudice Showing?

Adolph Hitler boasted at the end of his year of greatest triumphs: "God up to now has placed the stamp of approval on our battle . . . . The year 1941 will bring completion of the greatest victory of our history."

Hitler didn't know that God long ago spoke to Abraham some words to make Hitler's victory impossible. "I will make you a great nation . . . and I will bless those who bless you; and the one who curses you I will curse" (Gen. 12:2-3).

God was speaking of the Jewish nation, which Hitler had put his hand out to destroy. In doing so the Nazi leader doomed himself, for within a few short years, Hitler and his military might perished.

Haman's action was the first recorded effort to exterminate the Jews. Pharaoh had tried to limit their numbers by ordering the massacre of male babies. Various tribes in Canaan resisted the Jewish invasion. Nebuchadnezzar carried the nation away into captivity.

Haman rose fast to power by winning the king's favor (3:1). By order of Ahasuerus, Haman caused quite a stir when he passed through the busy gate of the citadel. Judges, government officials, and common folk alike dropped whatever they were doing to prostrate themselves on the dusty pavement of stone.

"When Haman saw that Mordecai neither bowed down nor paid homage to him, Haman was filled with rage" (3:5, NASB).

Haman hungrily craved all the honors he could extort. Likewise, Hitler craved the acclaim of the multitude. Perhaps Haman's sudden elevation made him insecure in his job. Some people work long and hard to attain greatness: After covering all intermediate steps, they feel comparatively sure of themselves in high position—sure enough to show magnanimity toward opponents.

But not Haman. In the stubborn Jew standing upright, perhaps Haman saw his own true worth mirrored. Mordecai's attitude made all Haman's honors and trappings shrivel.

Adolph Hitler came from a miserable background. In his early years a sense of degradation gnawed at his soul. He sought endlessly for deference and security. Along the way, he found relief in hatred of various groups, including Jews. Said he in *Mein Kampf*, as his hatred of Jews grew, "I was transformed from a weakly world-citizen into a fanatic anti-Semite."

We don't know Haman's background. We do know he showed a ridiculous need for appreciation. By ignoring Mordecai's slight, Haman could have continued as prime minister to the king of Persia. Instead he lost everything, even his life. As Haman climbed to the top, we see the seeds of his own destruction already planted within him.

Helga (not her real name) spent a lifetime struggling for attention. When she was three, her mother died, leaving a family of five children. The father spent most of his waking hours trying to earn a living. A stepmother felt all she could possibly do was take care of the children physically. Helga, lively and precocious, seemed particularly troublesome.

Helga grew up starved for attention. She learned how to earn it in legitimate ways. But she also laid burdensome demands upon those around her. Her life revolved around whether she would receive the gifts, cards, letters, telephone calls, invitations, and public mention she considered her due. People loved her, but worried constantly about missing some little attention she expected. She suffered tortures of rejection if someone lapsed in any way.

If you lavish sufficient love and attention on your little child, he'll get enough. He'll become able to move out freely into the everyday world. He won't find himself chained for a lifetime to the need for abnormal amounts of recognition.

"But he disdained to lay hands on Mordecai alone, for they had told him who the people of Mordecai were; therefore Haman sought to destroy all the Jews, the people of Mordecai, who were throughout the whole kingdom of Ahasuerus" (3:6, NASB).

The word "destroy" means literally "to wipe out." It occurs frequently in the Book of Esther. Haman could easily have rid himself of that one unyielding Jew. But he'd grown used to doing things on a tremendous scale, in the style of Xerxes. If Haman already hated Jews, learning Mordecai was a Jew only confirmed his prejudice. Or perhaps his reasoning leaped from the specific to the general. People do it all the time: "A waiter was very rude to me in France. I don't like Frenchmen." "I had a bad experience with a church member. I hate all churches.''

On the other hand, you help to form, or to dissipate, other people's prejudices. As you travel abroad, anyone who meets you evaluates Americans by how you act. We heard an American businessman in Pisa, Italy, booming out over a hotel lobby, ''The way to see Rome is by taxi. I saw the whole thing in four hours. Nothing worth looking at.''

What could Italians conclude about him? What might other Americans conclude about traveling businessmen? ''None of us liveth to himself'' (Rom. 14:7). Likewise the world will evaluate Christianity by what it sees in an individual.

Haman equated Mordecai with the whole Jewish race. Mordecai refused to bow down at the king's command. Therefore the whole race would likely break the law. If a whole nation had to perish for every wrongdoer, the earth would long since be empty of people.

God says we're to overcome prejudice in our hearts and put away all wrath, malice, and slander. We should be kind to one another: tenderhearted, forgiving each other, even as God for Christ's sake has forgiven us. (See Eph. 4:31-32.)

The Old Testament gives very careful instructions on how to treat the stranger—the person different from yourself. Don't do him any wrong; treat him as a native; love him as yourself (Lev. 19:33-34). The New Testament word for hospitality is ''love of strangers,'' *philoxenia* (Rom. 12:13).

Jesus said, ''Whatever you did for one of the least of these brothers of Mine, you did for Me'' (Matt. 25:40, NIV). He meant His brothers according to the flesh, the Jews; or brothers according to the Spirit, believers.

Haman, in his distorted vision, didn't see the hundreds

of humble artisans and craftsmen he knew, or the inof-fensive women and children. All he saw was one Jew who had insulted him.

Unwittingly, Mordecai brought a threat of disaster upon his whole nation.

"In the first month, that is the month Nisan, in the twelfth year of King Ahasuerus, they cast Pur, that is, the lot, before Haman from day to day, and from month to month, to the twelfth month, that is, the month Adar" (3:7).

Five years had passed since Esther became queen (2:16).

Haman paused to learn the most propitious time for wiping out the Jewish nation. It was Nisan, roughly April, first month of the year. Persians believed the gods at the first of each year came together to fix the fates of men. Haman called in soothsayers and watched. They cast stones, painted or carved with markings, like dice. Or they used pieces of wood, strips of papyrus, or parchment. The experts cast the lot for each day of the year to find the luckiest day.

But the Bible says God controls even the lot: "A lot is cast into a lap, but how it will come out is decided by the Lord" (Prov. 16:33, BECK). Haman had made his plans, leaving the God of Israel out of his calculations.

In the Old Testament some important things were decided by lot. It was used for the last time before Pentecost (Acts 1). Since Pentecost, we have the Holy Spirit for guidance.

The day settled upon turned out to be the best day for the Jewish cause and the worst day for Haman. The end of the year, Adar, or our March, was 11 months away. Even Haman's superstition was made to cooperate in the plan of God.

A Jewish commentator said the 11 months gave the Jews time to repent and be saved. It gave time for their rescue. The best time for Haman would have been immediately, with no warning at all, so that there was no chance for any means of deliverance to develop.

All ancient people submitted their plans to some kind of augury. Even today people recognize an element beyond their control in the outworking of events. They call it chance, or luck. The Book of Esther brings out this unknown element as Providence.

"And Haman said unto King Ahasuerus, 'There is a certain people scattered abroad and dispersed among the people in all the provinces of thy kingdom; and their laws are diverse from all people, neither keep they the king's laws: therefore it is not for the king's profit to suffer them'" (3:8).

Haman moved, as prejudiced people do, from fact to fiction. True, Jews were scattered throughout the entire Persian empire. A little knot of them had gone back to Jerusalem to rebuild the temple. But enough enemies surrounded even those Jews to do them in—given any official encouragement (Ezra 4:4-10). Assyria had deliberately sought to homogenize all peoples throughout the Empire. Haman implied that as a scattered nation, Jews would prove too weak to organize and defend themselves.

Persia, the conqueror of both Assyria and Babylon, allowed nations to keep their own religion and culture. Therefore Haman had to make a special case out of the Jews.

Haman said Jews refused to homogenize. People everywhere resented their aloofness. Their religion kept them separate, a nation within a nation. Haman correctly stated they held a distinctive body of law. Here, the

Book of Esther comes closest to referring to Mosaic Law. Haman seemed to understand more about it than he spoke of.

People felt insulted that Jews wouldn't eat any food but their own. Jews were always observing some Sabbath or holiday of their own. They ignored other people's holidays. They wouldn't accept other people's daughters in marriage, nor give their daughters. On the days people wanted to do business with them, they shut up shop. The days other people wanted to observe holidays, the Jews said were lawful days to do business.

Haman moved into fiction when he said they did not observe the laws of the Empire, so it was not in the king's interests to tolerate them. Jews have characteristically lived as law-abiding citizens. Many have made great contributions in government, business, and the professions. Jews who came to us in the time of Hitler enormously enriched our country, among them Albert Einstein and Henry Kissinger. Many started businesses that provided jobs for many other Americans.

Hitler only refined anti-Semitism into a political system. He didn't discover anything new for appealing to greed, narrowness, and pride. Hitler added his own ridiculous fictions to a few basic facts about the Jews. Unfortunately, the same fictions and lies are peddled today, even by some who call themselves Christians.

God intended the Law to make His people stand out in the world as witnesses to Himself, remarkable for their wisdom and understanding (Deut. 4:5-8). Somehow God's design became distorted.

"If it please the king, let it be written that they may be destroyed: and I will pay ten thousand talents of silver to the hands of those that have the charge of the business, to bring it into the king's treasuries" (3:9).

Although Haman appealed to greed, the king seems to decline the money offered by Haman (3:11). But Mordecai later knows where the money will go (4:7). Also Esther, when she said, "We have been sold" (7:4, NASB). Ahasuerus had lost interest in governing. He handed over power to Haman as readily as later he handed it to Mordecai. The people were at the mercy of whomever the king favored. Lives of other people meant nothing to him.

"And the king took his ring from his hand, and gave it unto Haman the son of Hammedatha the Agagite, the Jews' enemy" (3:10).

In handing over his signet ring, Ahasuerus gave Haman power to act in his name. In ancient times, only about as many people could write as can't write in our society. So the usual signature was made with a carved signet pressed into wax. Each individual's signet was distinctive and guarded as carefully as we watch what we sign.

We see the lines of conflict clearly drawn. Mordecai has been labeled "the Jew," and Haman "the enemy of the Jews."

Haman summoned the king's scribes and they wrote out the order, in the language each province could understand (3:12).

Haman proceeded to whip up anti-Semitism throughout the Empire. Joseph Goebbels, a Nazi propagandist, said Hitler's opportunity was to "unchain volcanic passions, to arouse outbreaks of fury, to set masses of men on the march, to organize hate and suspicion with ice-cold calculation." A Haman may be only a little person, without power, who spreads rumors against the Jews. Or he may be a Hitler who mobilizes a nation to murder and mass hysteria.

"And the letters were sent by posts into all the king's provinces, to destroy, to kill, and to cause to perish, all Jews, both young and old, little children and women, in one day . . . and to take the spoil of them for a prey" (3:13).

The Jews were to finance their own destruction, as well as enrich the treasury. All the wealth they held showed what income their abilities brought to the Empire.

Haman used the well-known Persian postal system, available for government missives only. Herodotus wrote, "Nothing mortal travels as fast as these Persian messengers . . . . Along the whole line of road there are men . . . stationed with horses . . . allowing a man and a horse to each day . . . and these men will not be hindered from accomplishing at their best speed the distance which they have to go, either by snow, or rain, or heat, or by the darkness of night" (8.98). It was an ancient pony express.

Our post office adapted these words from Herodotus to be carved in stone on the main post office in New York.

A message could go to the farthest regions of the Empire in two or three weeks. An ordinary traveler would require three months or more to cover the same distance.

The edict was published to all peoples so that they should be ready for the day (3:14). Haman wanted the order to go out fast. Perhaps he wanted the Jews to suffer in anticipation. Perhaps he wanted them to flee the country, leaving all possessions for confiscation by the government. But where could anyone go to escape from the Persian Empire?

"The posts went out, being hastened by the king's commandment, and the decree was given in Shushan the pal-

ace. And the king and Haman sat down to drink; but the city Shushan was perplexed'' (3:15).

Haman, cold and calculating, still sought to manipulate and distract the king. The perpetrators of the edict sat down to drink while the death sentence for Jews threw the whole city into a turmoil. Who, they might have wondered, would be annihilated next?

6
The Chance of a Lifetime

We all look for the spot in life where our efforts will count most.

When Annette (not her real name) visited a school for an interview, she saw children in wheelchairs. Others limped, some wore braces, and several walked on crutches. Some suffered from serious deformities.

Annette's heart reached out in understanding. She had learned to live triumphantly with her own malformation. For several years she had taught normal children. When they asked why her neck was that way, she simply stated, "That's the way God made me." They loved her blithe spirit and sparkling personality.

Annette heard of an opportunity to teach handicapped children and applied for the job. She got it, and in that work Annette discovered her calling in life. She found herself especially equipped to teach not only school subjects, but also courage and hope. In the midst of tragedy and sorrow, Annette found challenge and satisfaction.

Like Annette and many others, Esther found her great opportunity in the midst of suffering.

"When Mordecai perceived all that was done, Mordecai rent his clothes, and put on sackcloth with ashes, and went out into the midst of the city, and cried with a loud and a bitter cry" (4:1).

News of the edict to destroy all Jews hurled Mordecai into deepest mourning. He went about the streets of Susa wailing aloud, with torn garments. Hebrew and Persian alike understood. He was expressing grief. Women must have wearied of mending all those torn clothes. But convention required that people express despair by ripping apart their garments. Men and women alike acted out their grief.

Psychologists tell us that American men don't express their emotions enough. By stifling tears, they stifle other emotions, such as love and tenderness. Suffocation of feelings can also bring high blood presure, heart attacks, ulcers, and psychosomatic illnesses.

Mordecai put on sackcloth, made from the hair of goats, sometimes of camels, and usually black (compare Revelation 6:12). It was very uncomfortable to wear next to the skin. The same coarse material was sometimes used in sacks (Gen. 42:27). Our word for sack derives from the Greek *sakko*. In Hebrew the word is *saq*.

The ashes Mordecai sprinkled over himself signified what was valueless and loathsome. Ashes could express misery and shame. In the Old Testament ashes also expressed abasement and contrition before God. (See 2 Sam. 13:19; Job 2:8; Isa. 58:5; Dan. 9:3.)

So Mordecai might have been expressing strong feelings of reaching out to God. The Bible doesn't say. It only describes his outward actions.

Did Mordecai connect his mild act of independence with the outrageous consequences? If he did, he must have suffered a thousand times more than any other Jew.

He might wish he'd never seen Haman, that he'd gone back to Jerusalem, or that he'd chosen a simple life, away from kings and courts. Many a governmental figure, when attacked, must wish he'd chosen a less complicated life.

"And came even before the king's gate: for none might enter into the king's gate clothed with sackcloth" (4:2).

After parading his grief in the city, Mordecai went to the city square in front of the king's gate. Wealth and power couldn't shut out sorrow, even from a palace. But it could shut out displays of sorrow. Mordecai couldn't enter even the courtyard in sackcloth.

"And in each and every province, withersoever the king's commandment and his decree came, there was great mourning among the Jews, and fasting, and weeping, and wailing; and many lay in sackcloth and ashes" (4:3).

To the far reaches of the empire, Jews mourned. They also fasted. Every chapter so far has mentioned at least one feast: the six-month and seven-day feasts of Ahasuerus; the feast of Vashti; the feast celebrating Esther's elevation; the feast of Ahasuerus and Haman after sending out the terrible decree. In every succeeding chapter, feasting will hold a prominent place. But not in this chapter. Here, by contrast, we see widespread fasting among the Jews.

What did fasting mean to a Jew? To Americans it might mean only a desire to lose weight, or possibly a hunger strike with no religious connotation. But to a Jew, fasting ordinarily meant prayer, humbling oneself before God. Outside the Book of Esther, the Bible almost invariably links fasting with prayer. (See Judges 20:26; 1 Sam. 7:6; 2 Sam. 12:16; 1 Kings 21:27-29; 2 Chron. 20:3; Ezra 8:21; Neh. 1:4; Neh. 9:1-3; Ps. 35:13; Isa. 58:3-7; Jer. 14:12; Joel 1:14; 2:12-14; Jonah 3:5-9.)

The author avoided mentioning prayer. Yet when he spoke of fasting, the thought of prayer would immediately come into any Jew's mind. Likewise, in the rest of Esther the author deliberately avoided mentioning anything religious. Why? We don't know.

Perhaps Jews throughout the empire did take that dread decree as a judgment from God. Maybe they did turn to Him in grief and repentance, begging that the judgment be removed.

Back in the Land, that pattern occurred over and over again in the history of Israel. They would turn away from God. He'd allow an enemy to rise up against them. They'd repent of their sins, and turn back to God. He'd deliver them (Judges 2:10-23). In Esther we see God at work even among His scattered nation. "For whom the Lord loveth He correcteth; even as a father the son in whom He delighteth" (Prov. 3:12).

"So Esther's maids and her chamberlains came and told it her. Then was the queen exceedingly grieved; and she sent raiment to clothe Mordecai, and to take away his sackcloth from him: but he received it not" (4:4).

The people who served Esther by this time knew Mordecai meant something special to her. They may even have known she was Jewish, without conveying that knowledge to the king or Haman.

Esther too acted out her anguish. She knew Mordecai couldn't enter the palace courtyard dressed in sackcloth. So she sent garments that would allow him to enter.

Mordecai refused the garments. But he had succeeded

in arousing Esther's concern. Again we see the strong bond between Esther and Mordecai. Five years in the king's harem had not changed her feeling for her adoptive father.

"Then called Esther for Hatach one of the king's chamberlains, whom he had appointed to attend upon her, and gave him a commandment to Mordecai, to know what it was, and why it was" (4:5).

Esther couldn't go outside the gate, and Mordecai refused to change his garments to come in. Apparently his duties allowed him access to the inner court ordinarily (see 2:1).

"So Hatach went forth to Mordecai unto the street of the city, which was before the king's gate" (4:6).

Esther no doubt selected a eunuch she knew she could trust, perhaps a fellow Jew. He did what a messenger is supposed to do—conveyed the word faithfully, without adding to or taking from it. Thus we're to serve God as messengers, conveying His word faithfully.

"And Mordecai told him of all that had happened unto him, and of the sum of the money that Haman had promised to pay to the king's treasuries for the Jews, to destroy them" (4:7).

So the king was going to accept the money. (Compare 3:9.) Certainly, the war against Greece had depleted his coffers. Mordecai evidently possessed some kind of pipeline to the palace secrets. Such a staggering amount of money would convince anyone the Jewish cause was lost.

"Also he gave him the copy of the writing of the decree that was given at Shushan to destroy them, to shew it unto Esther, and to declare it unto her, and to charge her that she should go in unto the king, to make supplication unto him, and to make request before him for her people" (4:8).

Mordecai had gotten hold of a copy of the edict. He sent it to Esther. It looks as if Esther could read—a rare accomplishment in those days. We see here a hint of Mordecai's careful and devoted teaching throughout Esther's childhood. He appealed to her as a strong and intelligent woman, expecting the facts to speak for themselves. He knew Esther's concern for their people.

How could Mordecai order Esther? She now owed obedience only to her husband. Yet in every life a time comes when "We ought to obey God rather than men" (Acts 5:29). Mordecai had trained Esther to respect him as parent, to respect God even more. He believed he could command Esther on so important an issue. But would she respond to the order?

"And Hatach came and told Esther the words of Mordecai. Again Esther spake unto Hatach, and gave him commandment unto Mordecai" (4:9-10).

Esther respectfully sent back an objection to Mordecai's order: "All the king's servants, and the people of the king's provinces, do know, that whosoever, whether man or woman, shall come unto the king into the inner court, who is not called, there is one law of his to put him to death, except such to whom the king shall hold out the golden sceptre, that he may live: but I have not been called to come in unto the king these thirty days" (4:11).

The problem appeared insurmountable. Esther came up with an excellent excuse for not acting in the crisis. People could come to the outer court and present requests for an audience. But all requests would doubtless go through Haman. The rule protected the king from would-be assassins and dissatisfied subjects, including disgruntled wives and concubines. The king did the summoning.

History records many intrigues involving women of the harem. Courtiers did their best to weaken a queen's influence with the king. Esther certainly couldn't expect to go through regular channels. Her only possibility was to approach the king directly. She could only hope the sight of her would stir memories of past feelings. She felt her hold on the king slipping. Though living in another part of the same palace, he hadn't felt the need to see her for a month. Other wives or concubines had occupied the fickle king's attention.

Apparently, the luxury and idleness of the palace had ensnared Esther to a degree. She didn't immediately summon up courage to act. Difficulties loomed before her. She forgot the insurmountable obstacles God had already brought her past. How did she happen to live in this palace at all?

Some think Esther's fears make her less the heroine. They really make her more human. A rash person may do the brave thing without thinking of dangers involved. The really brave person acts, with full knowledge of the dangers.

"And they told to Mordecai Esther's words" (4:12).

Apparently, Hathach took someone else along with him, maybe as a witness, to guarantee the truth of what he relayed.

"Then Mordecai told them to reply to Esther, 'Do not imagine that you in the king's palace can escape any more than all the Jews. For if you remain silent at this time, relief and deliverance will arise for the Jews from another place and you and your father's house will perish. And who knows whether you have not attained royalty for such a time as this?'" (4:13-14, NASB)

Throughout history, people have asked themselves, and asked of others, that wonderful question addressed to Esther. "Who knoweth whether thou art come to the kingdom for such a time as this?" You see a need. You're on the spot. God has prepared you with the necessary abilities. You act, and know the supreme joy of having done what you could to right a wrong, or change the course of history.

Or you don't act, and suffer remorse for a lifetime. God finds someone else to accomplish His purposes. But you find yourself left out of the main stream of His directive will.

Mordecai applied just the right amount of pressure to produce the right kind of fear. He first appealed to Esther on a selfish level. He told her she couldn't hope to escape, even in the palace. Someone with a grudge would point her out as a Jew. Then he lifted Esther's sights. He helped her see her situation in the light of God's sovereignty in her life.

Why are you in your particular circumstance? What special opportunity does God offer you? Have you acted on it?

Pope John XXIII came to the top office of the Roman Catholic Church at a special time in history. Many devout souls were longing for an open Bible, a deeper walk with Christ, and a greater identity with other followers of Christ. He encouraged Bible study. Catholics went to

Bible classes or joined home Bible studies. Centuries-old walls came tumbling down.

Far off from Rome, I felt the effects of his courageous act. Dozens of Catholics attend my classes, often encouraged by priests and nuns. A Catholic college gave credit in "religion" to a woman who completed my course of study through the Bible—in a Protestant church. Likewise, Esther's act was felt to the far reaches of an empire.

In his appeal to Esther, Mordecai came close to stating a deep faith in God, as close as anywhere in the Book of Esther. He almost said God would never allow the Jewish people to perish.

Mordecai's words fully roused Esther. She grasped the danger, grasped the risk, grasped the opportunity, completely, and made her choice.

Sometimes we need to compel loved ones to face facts to rouse them to action. Sometimes we need a friend, a loved one to appeal to us even on the low level of self-preservation. We need to stir up each other to do what God expects.

"Then Esther bade them return Mordecai this answer, 'Go, gather together all the Jews that are present in Shushan, and fast you for me, and neither eat nor drink three days, night or day: I also and my maidens will fast likewise; and so will I go in unto the king, which is not according to the law: and if I perish, I perish'" (4:15-16).

Esther's choice was to die for certain in 11 months, or risk dying now. She undertook her responsibility with all the elation of a person going to a heart operation: possible death as against sure death.

But she undertook it, knowing all the risks. And she

put her trust in God. Fasting wouldn't improve her beauty. The way of the pagan harem was to apply fine creams, perfumes, and decide which clothes and jewelry to wear. Rest and proper foods were necessary for Esther to appear at her peak.

But Esther fasted. She placed her trust in God, not in the bloom in her cheeks. In the moment of decision, she became strong, not weak. She commanded Mordecai, and he accepted her direction. In any truly deep relationship each can be guided by the other, on occasion. Each can recognize when the other comes up with a strong message from God.

Esther told Mordecai to assemble all the Jews in Susa. Haman had told the king they were a people scattered, therefore weak. Esther knew they would gather to pray, strengthening her by their solidarity.

Esther said she and her maidens would likewise fast. How could she speak for the seven special maidens chosen for her? They were Persian maidens, no doubt, and high in rank. In those five years she must have conveyed to them something of her own personal faith in the Hebrew God.

Esther, even in a pagan king's harem, could make a choice and act for God. Even as did Abraham, though he wasn't always in the right spot. Even as did David, who kept a harem of wives and concubines. Many Old Testament heroes were imperfect. But if God could work only through perfect people, who would there be to do His work in the world?

"So Mordecai went his way, and did according to all that Esther had commanded him" (4:17).

Literally, he "crossed over." He crossed over the river flowing toward the Persian Gulf, the river separating the palace and its adjuncts on the acropolis from the city on the other side.

Mordecai had done what he could with Esther. He proceeded to summon the Jews in the city to assemble and fast.

7
Courage to Meet Your Crisis

Jim, who runs a book-distributing service for Christian literature, tells a wonderful experience of God's intervention.

"We'd been trying to get into a drugstore chain for a long time. We wrote letters, called on them, and got no response whatever.

"Then we decided to pray every day that the chain of 180 stores would open to us. We had prayed for about a month when the buyer called. He wanted to make an appointment for me to see him.

"When I went for that appointment, the buyer didn't take me into his own small office. Instead, he showed me into his boss's area. His boss was a vice-president of the chain.

"While sitting there, the buyer got called out for a long-distance phone call. That left me with the vice-president, Bill Jackson (not his real name). He proceeded to ask, 'Just what kind of books are you selling?'

"'Inspirational books,' I replied.

"'Does that include astrology, things like that?'

"'No, we don't believe in that. Just good Christian books.'

"'Good,' he said. Then he shared how he had come to know Christ only three weeks before. He had seen our proposal on the buyer's desk. It appealed to him, and he wanted to see our books in the stores. His whole family was Christian, he said. His wife had been praying he would come to know the Lord.

"Now our books are in every store of the chain, except six stores which are too small. Per square footage, we outsell the other books they carry. I've just learned that for next year we have 8 feet of shelf space, or 10 by 12 feet, depending on the store. We're built permanently into the floor plan for each outlet to follow.

"Since that time, Bill Jackson has continued to walk with the Lord, and continued to share with me. His career has taken off. He's now second in command in the whole chain. I believe God honors those who honor Him."

Jim, the Christian book distributor, depended upon God to open the way. He also used tact and shrewdness in presenting his cause. Persistently, he tapped along a seemingly solid wall to find God's breach in it. Then God opened the way before him.

Jim might have considered himself unable to change the policy of a mighty drugstore chain. "But . . . God hath chosen the weak things of the world to confound the things which are mighty" (1 Cor. 1:27). Jim trusted God.

Esther not only decided to put her life on the line for a cause. She also used all the skill she could muster to effect a successful outcome. She certainly considered herself one of the weak things of the world: left an orphan, a defenseless little girl; member of a subject race, now doomed. She was a queen among many wives and concubines, but without power even to approach the king. She had no way of knowing her current favor with him.

Yet God used her against the mightiest monarch of the day to deliver His people, thereby to show that the power was of Him. That's why God allows shortages, problems, and tight places in our lives. We learn day by day His power to deliver.

God worked through the beauty and shrewdness He gave Esther. She outwitted the king and his all-too-clever prime minister.

"Two days later Esther put on her royal dress and stood in the inner court of the king's palace, facing the king's hall. The king was sitting on his royal throne inside his palace, opposite the entrance" (5:1, BECK).

According to Jewish reckoning, three days meant part of the first day, the full second day, and part of a third day. Esther and her maids spent those days fasting, and by implication, praying. They were dressed, no doubt, in mourning garb as were the Jews whom Mordecai assembled to fast in Susa.

Fasting in the Old Testament suggested being so absorbed in prayer as to forget food. The other day a friend of mine left her house at 6:30 in the morning, without taking time to eat. She kept doing one thing after another all day till 8:30 at night without stopping to eat. Then she went home to a bowl of soup.

What do you get so absorbed in that you forget to eat? Some stay out fishing for hours after mealtime, especially if the fish are biting. Sometimes mothers become so absorbed in caring for needs they forget to eat; likewise doctors. A writer gets so absorbed in writing she forgets about eating till she suddenly feels faint. Sometimes even then she puts off stopping when she knows she should.

That's the kind of praying Esther and the other Jews were doing. In 10 months, time would run out for the whole nation. Eating didn't matter, compared to humbling themselves before God, confessing, repenting, and beseeching God to intervene and deliver them as He had done many times before, back in the Land. Fasting increased their sense of weakness and dependence upon God.

On the third day, Esther took off her mourning clothes and put on queenly garb. Not that she felt like dressing up, you can imagine. But having committed herself to her fearful undertaking, she intended, if possible, to carry it through with success. Esther showed no taste for useless martyrdom.

The Bible often mentions appropriate garb for an occasion. Esther knew she must look her best. Though her whole nation grieved in sackcloth and ashes, she must dress to capture the king's fancy a second time.

Most women will take the trouble to wear what pleases their husbands. (Compare Prov. 31:21-22; 1 Tim. 2:9-10.) All of us are to be dressed in God's robe of righteousness, in His garments of salvation (Isa. 61:10). Christ told the parable of the wedding guests who could not be admitted to the wedding. They lacked the proper garment, which was faith in Him (Matt. 22:1-14).

Esther approached the main entrance to the audience hall, open to the inner court. She violated the law in even coming to the inner court (4:11). You can stand at one end of the audience hall at Persepolis and imagine Esther's feelings. (Xerxes' audience hall at Persepolis, the summer palace, is similar to that at Susa, but better preserved.) Six rows of mighty columns dwarfed her. A ceiling beamed with cedar stretched above the great pillars. The walls were magnificently lined with glazed brick in many colors.

At the far end of the hall, on a raised platform some 250 feet away, sat the king, resplendent on his gold-covered throne, holding the gold-covered scepter. His trappings were designed to overawe and intimidate. Innumerable reliefs from the time show Persian kings in this very posture, always holding the scepter symbolic of their power.

The gold throne and the rich fabrics shimmered in the distance. Esther, faint from lack of food, breathlessly watched that scepter. Would it move—or must she die? Esther before Ahasuerus is a picture of the Jews of the diaspora; Ahasuerus is a symbol of worldly power bearing rule over God's chosen people. Yet today, Ahasuerus is only important to us because of his relationship to Esther. True worth dwelt in Esther.

"And it was so, when the king saw Esther the queen standing in the court, that she obtained favor in his sight: and the king held out to Esther the golden sceptre that was in his hand. So Esther drew near, and touched the top of the sceptre" (5:2).

The scepter moved, and Esther had to walk the enormous length of that hall. But at the end of it, she saw the scepter, as long as a man's height, extended for her to touch. Once again, her beauty bewitched him as it had five years before (2:17). "The king's heart is in the hand of the Lord, as the rivers of water: He turneth it whithersoever He will" (Prov. 21:1).

"Then said the king unto her, 'What wilt thou, Queen Esther? And what is thy request? It shall be even given thee to the half of the kingdom'" (5:3).

The king knew no trivial matter could have made Esther take such a risk. He asked for her request, making an extravagant promise. His promise expressed oriental politeness. (Compare Mark 6:23.) We also know Xerxes made other extravagant promises (Herodotus 9.109).

Esther, however, had decided not to blurt out her request before all those attendants. First, she would get the king into a mellow and amiable mood. Haman would be needed at hand to face up to her accusation. A little extra time would help build up her strength. She would need all the composure she could muster.

"And Esther answered, 'If it seem good unto the king, let the king and Haman come this day unto the banquet that I have prepared for him'" (5:4).

Esther understood the king's love of high living. She also knew how much he valued Haman. Maybe resentment of Haman on her part had made the king withdraw from her. The king seemed pleased that she invited his favorite. Maybe he thought it meant she accepted Haman at last.

"Then the king said, 'Cause Haman to make haste, that he may do as Esther hath said.' So the king and Haman came to the banquet that Esther had prepared" (5:5).

Esther's reluctance only made the king more curious. What did she want? When he finally learned, after so much delay, it might have seemed less than he expected. Wives, or husbands, might learn something from Esther about how to present a difficult request. She didn't rush in and overwhelm him. She waited for the right time, first reestablishing their relationship. Her request wasn't blurted out in irritation or condemnation.

The time for Esther to speak had not yet come. She had first to recapture the king's heart, not only with her beauty, but with her intelligence and good judgment. She planned to ask him to reverse a law of the kingdom.

"And, as they drank their wine at the banquet, the king said to Esther, 'What is your petition, for it shall be granted to you. And what is your request? Even to half of the kingdom it shall be done'" (5:6, NASB).

According to Persian custom, they lingered over the desserts and wine after the meal (Herodotus 1.133).

Esther had the king begging her to tell him what she wanted.

"Then answered Esther, and said, 'My petition and my request is. . . .'" (5:7)

She seemed to start to tell him. Then something stopped her. What? Intuition, as she studied the king's face? God's still small voice? We don't know. But we do know the iniquity of Haman was not yet complete. (Compare Gen. 15:16.) Often, evil must grow to full fruition before it can be dealt with. Did you ever have a doctor say, "We must wait till the problem gets worse before we can operate"?

In the next 24 hours Haman would build a gallows for hanging Mordecai, then make his ultimate reach for honor. In those same 24 hours the virtue of Mordecai would be brought strongly to the king's attention.

Then would come the right moment for Esther to speak. She'd know it. So she simply invited the king and Haman to another banquet (5:8) at which time she promised she would tell what was on her mind. She had time. Ten months for the Jews still remained.

"Then went Haman forth that day joyful and with a glad heart: but when Haman saw Mordecai in the king's gate, that he stood not up, nor moved for him, he was full of indignation against Mordecai" (5:9).

A stiff-backed individual, Mordecai certainly stood his ground. Whatever kept him from bowing down to Haman before still kept him upright. He sat firmly in his place of responsibility at the gate. Worst of all to Haman, Mordecai didn't even tremble. Even with his life and that of every Jew in the Empire doomed to end, he maintained his quiet confidence.

Haman went out puffed up by Esther's invitation like a porcupine with its quills sticking out. Yet he controlled himself during Mordecai's insult. At home, he indulged in preening before wife and friends.

"And Haman told them of the glory of his riches, and the multitude of his children, and all the things wherein the king had promoted him, and how he had advanced him above the princes and servants of the king" (5:11).

Some wives spend a lifetime propping up their husbands' weak egos. They must listen to endless bragging about their feats and accomplishments. If they can understand that such boasting comes from lack of confidence, giving the men the support they need may keep the men from so obviously asking for it.

A psychiatrist said if he could choose just one psychological quality for his children's future mates, he would choose a strong ego. A person with a strong ego can overlook slights. He doesn't live for other people's opinions of him. He doesn't have to squeeze praise and appreciation from those around him.

Poor Haman suffered from a weak ego. Affronted by

Mordecai, he tried to ease his pain by seeking adulation from his wife and friends.

"Haman said moreover, 'Yea, Esther the queen did let no man come in with the king unto the banquet that she had prepared but myself; and tomorrow am I invited unto her also with the king'" (5:12).

Haman's craving for recognition reduced his judgment. He imagined he had truly arrived at the peak of power. Not only had he caught the king in his web, but he fancied he had also captured the queen.

Some people spend a lifetime worrying about where they're invited or not invited. All of us know groups of people we wish would include us. Yet they don't. How wonderful that we can be guaranteed an invitation to the most important banquet of all, the Marriage Supper of the Lamb, by being members of His church, through faith in Christ! (Rev. 19:9)

"Yet all this availeth me nothing, so long as I see Mordecai the Jew sitting at the king's gate" (5:13).

The flaw for Haman was irritation over one person's attitude. Every situation, however glamorous or exalted, includes its Mordecai: the mosquitoes at a picnic; the leak in a mansion's roof; the office boy or stenographer with judgmental eyes; the peer you passed up on the job; the boss you can't stand.

"Then said Zeresh his wife and all his friends unto him, 'Let a gallows be made of 50 cubits high, and tomorrow speak thou unto the king that Mordecai may be hanged thereon: then go thou in merrily with the king unto the banquet'" (5:14).

"Stop complaining and act," said Haman's toadies. "If you're so all-powerful you can certainly rid yourself of a minor annoyance like Mordecai. Ease your discomfort right now by building a gallows high enough to be seen over the city wall."

"The thing pleased Haman; and he caused the gallows to be made" (5:14).

Many a wife or friend gives equally bad advice: fire your employee; complain to the boss; threaten to resign; get your former peer fired.

If you act on the advice, you may find your resignation accepted, a valuable employee lost, or a person fired who could really help you do your job.

Sometimes a person needs to be told, "Ignore the slight. It's no more important than a mosquito buzzing about in a banquet room. Don't wreck the banquet trying to swat the mosquito."

Their advice appealed to Haman's weakness and vanity. It encouraged him to make the final reach for power that helped put him in his grave, stripped of all honor and property.

The crisis point of the drama is reached, and it seems nothing can avert the impending tragedy for Mordecai. The gallows stand ready for him. Esther's plea still hangs in the balance. The Jews' fate remains unknown.

8
When Sleeplessness Saved a Life

The king couldn't sleep. Likewise, 15 percent of all Americans complain of insomnia, 50 percent of people over 50 years of age. More patients complain to their doctors about sleeplessness than about any other ailment.

All the king's wealth couldn't help him sleep. Americans spend millions every year on what they hope will help them sleep. Sales of hypnotics and tranquilizers have increased enormously in the United States over the past generation. Even while use of other drugs has increased only moderately. Yet the medical profession admits that all sleeping pills lose their power after several weeks of steady use. The head of a sleep disorders clinic even says the pills tend to *cause* insomnia if taken more than a few days or weeks. The brain overcompensates for the presence of the drug and negates its short-term effectiveness.

"On that night could not the king sleep, and he commanded to bring the Book of records of the Chronicles; and they were read before the king" (6:1).

King Ahasuerus couldn't command sleep, though he could command the wealth and labor of an empire. To this day, no reliable cure for sleeplessness exists. Still, insomniacs spend millions trying to sleep. They spend money on water beds, eye shades, ear plugs, air purifiers, yoga, and sauna baths. Doctors are experimenting with electro-sleep therapy, biofeedback, and hypnosis to help patients relax.

Some people solve the problem with commonsense remedies. Tests have shown that a 15-minute walk can have a more tranquilizing effect than a tranquilizer. Researchers say the body can't relax until the muscles become tired. So people exercise—some, diligently. Doctors also say that following a regular schedule encourages sleep. The Bible says, "The sleep of a laboring man is sweet" (Ecc. 5:12). He enjoys the blessing of tired muscles.

Many people have noticed they grow drowsy after a heavy steak dinner, or a cup of warm milk at bedtime. Experiments have shown that beef, milk, and other protein foods contain an amino acid that encourages sleep. Likewise, the calcium in milk helps nerves to relax.

Some people discover they don't need much sleep. A friend told me all she needs is four hours. When in the hospital having a baby, she hated lying in the dark all those hours. At home she simply gets up at three or four o'clock and cleans the house or bakes cookies. She has finished all her housework by the time other people wake up.

Others who need the rest know they must stay in bed. Like Ahasuerus, they figure out how they can use the time profitably. A minister works out outlines and illustrations for his sermons while lying awake for an hour or two. Others review their past, evaluate the present, or plan for the future. Keeping a pad and flashlight pen

handy to jot things down can help you get back to sleep;
you won't stay awake trying to remember things you
need to do, or good ideas that you fear might get away.

Ahasuerus called for records of the kingdom to be read
to him. Many insomniacs keep books handy to read
away the wakeful hours. They too pick a relaxing type of
reading matter. Ahasuerus probably hoped the droning
voice of the reader would make him grow drowsy.

David, the Psalmist, meditated, "When I remember
Thee upon my bed, and meditate on Thee in the night
watches; because Thou hast been my help, therefore in
the shadow of Thy wings will I rejoice" (Ps. 63:6-7).

The Bible seems to say that God controls even our
sleep. Sometimes you can get to sleep as you remember,
"He giveth His beloved sleep" (Ps. 127:2). And maybe
sometimes He's keeping you awake to tell you, "Now is
the accepted time; behold, now is the day of salvation"
(2 Cor. 6:2). You might find yourself some night totally
unable to sleep until you have accepted Christ as Sav-
iour, and settled things with God.

Ahasuerus' sleeplessness proved the turning point in
the fortunes of Haman and Mordecai. The Hebrew says,
literally, the chronicles "were being read" to Ahasuerus
over a period of time, apparently to early morning.

*"And it was found written, that Mordecai had told of
Bigthana and Teresh, two of the king's chamberlains,
the keepers of the door, who sought to lay hands on the
King Ahasuerus"* (6:2).

Three little verses, slipped into the account at the end of
chapter 2, suddenly become important. Mordecai had
done what he considered right—and reported a conspir-
acy against the king's life. He received nothing for it,
although such a service to the king would normally have

entitled him to an enormous reward or promotion. Yet, while Mordecai went on with his regular responsibility at the gate, he saw Haman getting all the promotions.

How many good deeds have you done for which you felt insufficiently rewarded? The Bible says none of your efforts are wasted. God keeps an account, whether men do nor not. Jesus said that even a cup of cold water given in His name would not fail to be rewarded (Matt. 10:42; Mark 9:41). "And the dead were judged out of those things which were written in the books, according to their works . . . . And they were judged every man according to his works" (Rev. 20:12-13).

Why was Mordecai's reward overlooked at the time? Because God was saving it up for the moment of supreme danger. At the right time God would bring it to the mind of the king. Mordecai's experience should make us patient about good efforts seemingly forgotten. We can safely hand over to the Lord all matters of reward.

"And the king said, 'What honor and dignity hath been done to Mordecai for this?' Then said the king's servants that ministered unto him, 'There is nothing done for him'" (6:3).

Xerxes considered it a point of honor to recompense outstanding service (Herodotus 3.138, 140; 5.11; 8.85, 90; 9.107; Thucydides *History of the Peloponnesian War* 1.138). It was also a matter of safety to reward anyone who protected his life. He certainly couldn't sleep with that obligation on his mind. He must act, instantly. Being a king, he could command action even at that hour of early morning.

"And the king said, 'Who is in the court?' Now Haman was come into the outward court of the king's house, to

speak unto the king to hang Mordecai on the gallows that he had prepared for him" (6:4).

All action focuses on Mordecai. The king couldn't wait till morning to reward him. Haman couldn't wait till morning for permission to have him hanged.

"And the king's servants said unto him, 'Behold, Haman standeth in the court.' And the king said, 'Let him come in'" (6:5).

No doubt, Haman felt flattered at the king's willingness to see him at such an early hour, and, apparently, in his bedchamber. Haman must have felt sure his request in regard to Mordecai would prove only a formality.

"So Haman came in. And the king said unto him, 'What shall be done unto the man whom the king delighteth to honor?' Now Haman thought in his heart, 'To whom would the king delight to do honor more than to myself?'" (6:6)

Haman swelled up like a seedpod ready to burst. One question from the king, and he gave vent to flights of fancy. His self-centeredness made him a poor advisor. He never stopped to inquire who the person was, or what might prove a meaningful reward for that person. Have you ever received a gift that was exactly what the giver wanted for himself—a gift ridiculously inappropriate for you? That's what Haman proposed. He alone occupied the highest position in the land, next to the king. Anyone else would prefer a promotion, or some tangible gift.

"Then Haman said to the king, 'For the man whom the king desires to honor, let them bring a royal robe which

the king has worn, and the horse on which the king has ridden, and on whose head a royal crown has been placed; and let the robe and the horse be handed over to one of the king's most noble princes and let them array the man whom the king desires to honor and lead him on horseback through the city square, and proclaim before him, "Thus it shall be done to the man whom the king desires to honor"''' (6:7-9, NASB).

Haman pictures the one thing more the king could have given him, short of the kingship. It was to let him ride around the streets on one of the king's horses, dressed in the king's clothes. Those handsome steeds, a special breed of Persia, are pictured in relief at Persepolis.

Wearing a king's clothing was considered the highest honor in the ancient Orient. (Compare Gen. 41:38-41; 1 Sam. 18:4; 1 Kings 1:33; also Herodotus 3.84; 7.116.) Surely the king must have guessed Haman was dreaming up all this for himself. What more could he ask short of the kingship itself? Perhaps at this moment Haman's words planted a seed of distrust in the king's mind.

To earlier translators, the crown on the horse's head was a problem. How could a horse wear a crown? It sounded ridiculous. Yet that's how the text plainly read. Recently, excavations have brought to light many royal horses with their manes woven into crown-like ornaments. Examples appear in reliefs on the walls of Xerxes' throne room at Persepolis.

Haman wanted the horse led not by some ordinary groomsman. He desired one of the king's most noble princes to conduct him through the streets, proclaiming honor to him before all people of the city.

"Then the king said to Haman, 'Make haste, and take the apparel and the horse, as thou hast said, and do even

so to Mordecai the Jew, that sitteth at the king's gate: let nothing fail of all that thou hast spoken'" (6:10).

The pod bursts. Feathery seeds of pride and vanity scatter. Haman stands there like a hollow shell, dumbfounded with shock. He must walk through the streets leading the horse of the man he wanted hanged.

Surely the king must have noticed the color drain from Haman's face.

Apparently, the king did not connect Mordecai the Jew with the unnamed people in 3:8. He'd been kept totally in the dark as to what was going on.

"Then took Haman the apparel and the horse, and arrayed Mordecai, and brought him on horseback through the street of the city, and proclaimed before him, 'Thus shall it be done unto the man whom the king delighted to honor'" (6:11).

Haman, ever acting in his own interest, knew he must obey the king. The whole project of getting Mordecai hanged lay dead. God can make your greatest enemy a means of advancing your interests. Whom then, should you fear, except God?

Up to this point, the fortunes of Haman, the enemy of the Jews, had been rising. Those of Mordecai, the Jew, had been going down.

In this chapter we reach the turning point of the story. Haman's and Mordecai's fortunes become reversed. And those reversals turn on a seeming triviality—the king's sleeplessness. Yet think of all the events in life that do turn on seeming trivialities. Apparently, God works through everyday happenings.

Haman's fortunes start downward; Mordecai's take an upward swing. Their reversals illustrate a law of life which Jesus put into words: "For whosoever exalteth himself shall be abased; and he that humbleth himself shall be exalted" (Luke 14:11).

If you haven't seen God's hand in events so far, you certainly see it here. Who but God could have caused so many streams of action to come together?

"And Mordecai came again to the king's gate" (6:12).

Imagine how ridiculous the whole proceeding appeared to Mordecai. He and his people were doomed to death. In the city, he would pass posters proclaiming the day of their doom. He would see Jews mourning in sackcloth and ashes. He would see the gallows that Haman had erected for him, Mordecai.

Yet, to be singled out for such honor must have given him a glimmer of hope. Maybe God was beginning to intervene in behalf of His people. Still, how much more Mordecai would have preferred to have been asked what he wanted!

At last it was all over, really adding up to nothing. Mordecai went back to his responsibility at the gate, as solemnly concerned for the Jews as before, not elated by what had happened.

"But Haman hasted to his house, mourning, and having his head covered" (6:12).

By contrast, Haman, unduly elated by success and unduly deflated by failure, lived for the opinions of others. His self-centeredness made him miserable at the height of good fortune. The trivial slight of Mordecai spoiled his happiness when he possessed everything. Now, because he had to honor someone else, he suffered so much he couldn't even show his face. Covering the head expressed the utmost depth of misery. (Compare 2 Sam. 15:30; 19:4; Jer. 14:3-4; Ezek. 24:17.)

But I do like the fact that he hurried home. He showed himself to be human in wanting to go home and hide. I do see good communication between Haman and his wife. He shared with her not only his good fortune, but also related the things that went against him.

"And Haman told Zeresh his wife and all his friends everything that had befallen him" (6:13).

One wife said to me, "I know my husband is having troubles in his business. He thinks he's protecting me by not telling me what's happening. But I'm miserable. By not talking about what's on his mind, he's not communicating at all. I feel shut out. I'd like to share whatever he's going through."

"Then said his wise men and Zeresh his wife unto him, 'If Mordecai be of the seed of the Jews, before whom thou hast begun to fall, thou shalt not prevail against him, but shalt surely fall before him'" (6:13).

Haman communicated, but Zeresh didn't prove the best counselor. After all, she and his friends put Haman up to erecting the gallows. Now they spoke honestly to him and offered absolutely no hope or comfort. Nor did they take any responsibility for their bad advice. In fact, they seemed to regard him already as a lost cause. No longer did they even bother to pander to his vanity. There was no further advantage for themselves in doing so.

What made Zeresh and the friends aware of God's special concern for Jews? Their words about the Jews, coming from non-Jews, seem very strong. Were they impressed by Cyrus' decree, and the Jews who had gone back to Jerusalem? Did they remember Daniel and his exploits in the court of Belshazzar of Babylon? Or Daniel in the court of Darius, Xerxes' father? Had these wise men read the history of the Jews, as told in the Jewish sacred writings? Did they know something of God's miraculous deliverances in the past?

We don't know. But we do know that the Old Testament made very clear that no one could destroy the Jewish nation, however scattered and weak. God said His covenant to preserve Israel could not be broken, anymore than man could change the sequence of day and night (Jer. 33:20-21).

Hitler destroyed six million Jews, but subsequently, a modern Jewish nation took shape. After Hitler, the Jewish people have become stronger than they have been since ancient times.

"And while they were yet talking with him, came the king's chamberlains, and hasted to bring Haman unto the banquet that Esther had prepared" (6:14).

As an important person, Haman was escorted without delay to the banquet. Only yesterday, the invitation had lifted his expectations to dizzy heights. Now the banquet had lost all its appeal. He went, but with foreboding.

9
You Reap What You Sow

The law of inevitable consequences is written into the universe. Lord Byron, the English poet, discovered this law in his own life. He threw his life away in immorality and reveling, and was cut short in his 30s. He wrote:

The thorns which I have reap'd
   are of the tree
I planted—they have torn me—and I
   bleed;
I should have known what fruit would spring
   from such a seed.

"Childe Harold's Pilgrimage," 4th Canto. Stanza 10, lines 88-90.

The idea of retribution shows up in folktales from Zanzibar to the Ozarks. Greeks, Romans, and Saxons believed man gets a just reward for his deeds. Bushmen, Buddhists, Moslems, and Brahmans believe in a justice at the heart of the universe, which will be operative in the next life if not in this.

Jews and Christians see the principle stated time and time again in Holy Writ. "Be not deceived; God is not mocked: for whatsoever a man soweth, that shall he also reap.'' (See Gal. 6:7.)

Haman sowed to the flesh; he reaped death. *Delay* in penalties doesn't mean the law has been abolished.

"So the king and Haman came to banquet with Esther the queen" (7:1).

The final banquet of Haman took place in a room overlooking a garden. The garden lay between the harem complex and the king's private apartments. Haman is a picture of evil people at the table of fortune, inflated with ambition, hot with envy, and bursting with hate.

Up to that point Haman had succeeded in his relentless quest for power. In the end, however, there was no deliverance for Haman, or anyone else, from the consequences of his own rebellion. God leaves such people as they prefer to be left, to pile wood for their own burning. God never interferes with human liberty.

God allows evil results to follow evil deeds (Isa. 45:7). He allows wretchedness, adversity, afflictions, and calamities to exist as results of sin.

The cruel person breeds enemies by his cruelty. Sometimes those enemies destroy him in retaliation. The vain person is punished by resentments he rouses in other people. Meanness is punished by hatred. Lying is punished by the distrust it builds. Coldness is punished by the indifference of other people.

All around us we see an indestructible connection between the violation of law and consequent misery. The mother must teach the little child that fire burns.

A ranger in a national park was telling us about mushrooms in the forest. Certain species kill, and she told of a man with an M.A. degree in botany, specializing in mushrooms. He ate the wrong kind and died, despite all his knowledge. She advised us to confine our mushroom eating to those grown commercially for food. We could take her warning or not, as we chose. God gives us ample warnings, which we can follow or not, as we choose. Bart and I chose not to eat even one of the beautiful mushrooms growing by the path in that forest.

The writer of Proverbs warned, "Whoso diggeth a pit shall fall therein" (26:27). We can expect to see Haman fall into the pit he dug for Mordecai.

"And the king said again unto Esther on the second day at the banquet of wine, 'What is thy petition, Queen Esther? And it shall be granted thee: and what is thy request? And it shall be performed, even to the half of the kingdom'" (7:2).

Good consequences tend to follow good acts. Follow the laws of health, and you'll be healthier than if you didn't. Work diligently, and you'll more likely succeed than if you laze through life. Love, and you'll more likely be loved. Give, and more is likely to be given you (Luke 6:36-38). The response you get back from other people tends to mirror what you give.

"Seek, and you'll find." Jesus gave that as a promise (Matt. 7:7-8; Luke 11:9-10).

Esther sought the good of her people. She chose to spend her life, if necessary, in an effort to save her nation. She and Mordecai received life and honor.

Jesus did give His life, a ransom for many. God accepted the offer. And Jesus received exaltation, an eternal weight of glory (Phil. 2:5-11).

The king, Esther, and Haman reclined at the banquet table. In the Persian custom, they lingered at table with fruit or dessert and wine, pleasantly relaxed. Once again, the king pressed Esther for her request. Esther knew at last the proper moment had come. Further delay could prove dangerous. She felt it as acutely as a modern money-raiser or salesman with his after-dinner sales talk.

The Jewish orphan girl at that moment held the heart of the king of Persia in her power. God had placed her in a certain position. He equipped her with beauty, charm, and tact. He let her choose whether to use her gifts for her people, or only for herself.

"Then Queen Esther answered and said, 'If I have found favor in your sight, O king, and if it please the king, let my life be given me as my petition, and my people as my request'" (7:3, NASB).

Esther carried the terrible burden in her heart of what she must ask for. But how should she say it?

The writer of Proverbs said, "A man may plan what he's going to say, but what he says comes from the Lord" (16:1, BECK). Man can plan his thoughts, but God gives the words. The best speeches are those for which you don't know all the words ahead of time. You study diligently. You plan your thoughts. You decide on your focus. But you leave the final form for the Holy Spirit to give when you face your audience.

Jesus promised the Holy Spirit would give the words. When you stand before important people, He says, don't worry. The Holy Spirit will teach you what you ought to say (Luke 12:11-12).

First God gave Esther the emotional strength to carry through two banquets cheerfully. Then He gave her exactly the right words to speak to Ahasuerus. She followed the proper formula for addressing a king, "If it please the king . . . " (Compare 1:19; 3:9; 5:4, 8; 8:5; Neh. 2:5.)

Esther approached the subject on a level the kind

could understand—loss of the beautiful woman reclining before him. He had already demonstrated that the death of a whole segment of his population wouldn't affect him. She didn't demand; she didn't accuse; she only appealed. She knew the king's imperious nature. He could swat her like a fly, as he had Vashti. She said nothing to hint at his part in Haman's vile scheme. She let the king save face.

Esther put her request modestly. She only asked for what she already had. She spoke in terms of the king's best interests.

In requesting her own life, Esther flung out the information that she was a Jew. Now, when it counted, she cast her lot firmly with her people.

Esther not only committed herself in a moment of fervor (4:16)—she also carried through her commitment to success. The drama of Esther by no means ends with the famous words, "If I perish, I perish."

Knowing she had the king's ear, Esther blurted it all out, "For we are sold, I and my people, to be destroyed, to be slain and to perish" (7:4).

Sold. Haman knew, and the king knew, about the bargain for the Jewish people—10,000 talents to be paid into the king's treasuries (3:9, 11; 4:7). Haman, at least, would recognize the exact wording of the edict: "destroyed . . . slain . . . perish."

So much hung on Esther's courage! She must attempt to reverse by mere weight of personal influence the decree of an empire. And that empire prided itself on infallibility. But the lions in her way proved chained and harmless. God was with her. What lions in your way have proved harmless?

Esther pushed on, utterly meek before the king. She didn't look to any kind of force to win her way. How many times an appeal will win, where a demand loses!

Almighty meekness is described over and over again in the Bible. (See Matt. 5:3-12, 38-45; John 18:36; Eph. 4:31-32; 2 Cor. 12:9.)

"If our men and women had only been sold to be slaves, I would have kept silent because such a distress would not be enough to trouble the king about it" (7:4 BECK).

Esther said she wouldn't have troubled the king about a mere change in social status. Though politically a captive people, the Jews lived as free citizens. They contributed to the wealth of the Empire through their work as artisans, farmers, clerks, and business people. If sold into slavery, they would continue to serve the king. But if the Jews were killed, the king would suffer serious loss of income.

"Then the King Ahasuerus answered and said unto Esther the queen, 'Who is he, and where is he, that durst presume in his heart to do so?'" (7:5)

The king recoiled in shock. Esther answered his first query, "A foe and an enemy." She answered his second question, "This wicked Haman" (7:6).

Why had Esther invited Haman? To the Oriental, hospitality meant a sacred act of friendship. Was it fair, to invite him only to accuse him? Yet she couldn't risk his getting a chance to misrepresent her case to the king. It was safest to face him in the presence of the king.

Esther didn't accuse Haman behind his back. If he had anything to say for himself, he could have said it. But Haman's own heart condemned him. He knew he had deliberately deceived the king. "Then Haman was afraid before the king and the queen" (7:6).

Esther's words hit the king like poisoned arrows.

Haman's guilt was betrayed by the terror written on his face. The mellow mood of the banquet exploded.

"And the king arising from the banquet of wine in his wrath went into the palace garden: and Haman stood up to make request for his life to Esther the queen; for he saw that there was evil determined against him by the king" (7:7).

The king rushed out to the garden. Perhaps his action expressed a desire to escape the terrible decision. He must decide between his wife and his favorite.

His favorite had deceived him, carried out a plot under his very eyes. The wakeful night had brought to his attention that the man who saved his life was a Jew. Haman wanted to kill all Jews, including Mordecai and Esther. Did that mean Haman had been in confederacy with those who conspired against the king? (2:21-23) Did he wish to avenge their death? Was the king even safe any longer with Haman alive?

Haman quickly sized up the situation, and saw Esther in command. Only she could save his life. He fell down at her couch in an agony of pleading. The man who so blithely ordered the death of thousands shriveled. Faced with his own death, he became a sniveling coward. Haman expressed no remorse, even to the extent that Judas did (Matt. 27:4). Only one thing concerned him now—his life.

The Middle-Eastern custom for petitioning suggests he might have been seizing Esther's feet, even kissing them. (See 8:3; 1 Sam. 25:24; 2 Kings 4:27; also frequently in Assyrian inscriptions.) Or perhaps when the king came back Haman tried to stand up and accidentally fell on Esther's couch.

"When the king came back from the palace garden into

*the palace where they'd been drinking wine, Haman was
lying on the couch where Esther was. 'Is he even going
to rape the queen in my presence, here in the palace?'
the king asked''* (7:8, BECK).

Palace etiquette defined very strictly how close anyone
could come to a royal concubine. Haman had over-
stepped the bounds even of common decency. Yet the
king certainly knew Haman was not at that moment making love to Esther.

*"As the word went out of the king's mouth, they covered
Haman's face"* (7:8).

Attendants began carrying out the death sentence by covering Haman's head.

Haman couldn't stand to have one Jew not bow down
to him. Now he had prostrated himself before a Jew to
beg for his life. The Bible says the time will come when
those who belong to Satan will bow at the feet of a re-
deemed Israel. Then will they know that God has loved
Israel (Rev. 3:9; also Isa. 49:23). In the meantime, the
truths of Esther lie hidden to an unredeemed world. An
unbeliever can read Esther and not see God in it at all.
But Jews know that experiences recounted in Esther have
occurred over and over again, throughout their sad and
remarkable history.

Should Esther have asked mercy for the enemy of the
Jews? How could she? If she spared Haman to continue
his machinations, she and her people might have perished. She didn't yet know the king's decision. The old
principle of an eye for an eye held.

*"And Harbonah, one of the chamberlains, said before
the king, 'Behold also, the gallows 50 cubits high, which*

Haman had made for Mordecai, who had spoken good for the king, standeth in the house of Haman.' Then the king said, 'Hang him thereon'' (7:9).

Harbonah was one of the eunuchs commanded to bring Vashti to the king (1:10). One of those who suggested the search for a new queen (2:2). He had been sent to escort Haman to the banquet (6:14). At that time he could have seen the gallows outside Haman's house. Evidently, Haman made no secret of its intended use.

Haman in power could command outward rites of respect. He hadn't bothered to make friends of those beneath him. Harbonah saw him slipping over the precipice out of the king's favor. He felt only too happy to give Haman a shove.

Perhaps Mordecai's unassuming nature commended him to palace attendants. Harbonah obviously wanted to see Haman on the gallows rather than Mordecai. Deftly he put the idea of hanging Haman into the king's mind. Again we see the king batted like a ping-pong ball. This time Esther won. The ball landed in Haman's court, and he couldn't return it. No attendant spoke up in favor of Haman. No one even urged delay.

"So they hanged Haman on the gallows that he had prepared for Mordecai. Then was the king's wrath pacified" (7:10).

All unknowingly, the king acted as God's instrument of justice for Haman. Evil had grown fully ripe.

Why does God wait so long to execute justice? Perhaps He wants to give the Hamans of this world full opportunity to turn, and repent—if they will. God gave Haman plenty of warning. Haman could have seen himself honestly, if he'd wanted to, through the eyes of

Mordecai. If he'd asked himself *why* Mordecai didn't want to bow down to him, Haman might have learned something.

Actually, Haman might have survived and kept his position if he had only ignored Mordecai's slight. But such people bring about their own ruin. Sooner or later they take the fatal misstep.

Adolph Hitler, puffed up with pride in his conquests, invaded Russia. But he couldn't fight a war on two fronts. His own act doomed him, as had Haman's.

"Though the mills of God grind slowly,
   yet they grind exceeding small".
   Friedrich von Logau, "Retribution"

10
Reverse the Irreversible?

Good and evil wage an age-long battle against each other, so the Bible says. Look around, and you'll see it. Everywhere, the struggle goes on.

Dorothy, hungry for spiritual things, attended a weekday Bible class. She accepted Christ, and became very excited about sharing her faith with her husband and neighbors. But her husband turned a deaf ear and neighbors resented her enthusiasm. Finally, her husband ordered her to stop attending the class.

To his surprise, she did. On every previous issue, she had fought him. Friends brought her tapes of the class, but she did not attend. After a few months, her husband softened. He said it was OK to attend the class if she wanted to. In time he became a Christian. Today, they enjoy a shared devotion to Christ and the church.

You can combat evil in various ways: force, direct resistance, hard work, scheming and planning, appeal, submission and suffering, risk or sacrifice, or love.

Dorothy used a combination of love and submission. She suffered at the time, but, "A soft answer turneth away wrath" (Prov. 15:1). Jesus said, "Blessed are the meek [or humble, gentle] for they shall inherit the earth" (Matt. 5:5).

The Book of Esther shows various ways in which God combats evil through His own. Esther used the soft approach.

Mordecai tried spurning evil. He detested Haman and all he stood for. He refused to extend to Haman the ordinary courtesies due his position. But Mordecai's action and attitude only stirred up worse trouble.

Mordecai then turned to scheming and planning. He appealed to the king through Esther. He apparently trusted God for deliverance (4:14), but at the same time exerted himself. He stirred up Esther to act. He gathered the Jews together to fast and, by implication, to pray.

Esther first tried risk or sacrifice for her people. The writer of Hebrews lists those who risked and came out on top; among them, Abraham, Joseph, and Moses. But, says the same writer, "Others experienced mockings and scourgings . . . chains and imprisonment. They were stoned . . . put to death . . . went about . . . destitute, afflicted, and ill-treated . . . (11:36-38). Yet God counted them victors and rewarded them accordingly.

We read in chapter 8 that Esther used appeal. Haman was dead. But the evil which Haman concocted lived on. The edict against her people still stood.

"On that day did the King Ahasuerus give the house of Haman the Jews' enemy unto Esther the queen" (8:1).

In Persia, any person who forfeited his life to the state automatically forfeited his estate. We might deplore Zeresh's losing not only her husband but also his property. Yet here too we see justice. She put him up to erecting the gallows for Mordecai (5:14). The king gave the estate to Esther, perhaps in compensation.

"And Mordecai came before the king; for Esther had told what he was unto her" (8:1).

Mordecai now became one of those few great men who could come into the king's presence (compare 1:10, 13-14; 7:9). He rose to recognition on his own merits in disclosing the plot against the king. But the mystery of Providence brought him to the king's attention at exactly the right moment (see 6:1-3).

Esther told the king not only of her blood relationship, but also of Mordecai's relationship to her as a father. Esther didn't outgrow gratitude for her good upbringing. The king must have felt gratitude to this man for making Esther what she was. We can always be grateful to those who made people we love what they are.

"And the king took off his ring, which he had taken from Haman, and gave it unto Mordecai" (8:2).

In the ruins at Persepolis a ring was found similar to the one Ahasuerus must have handed to Mordecai. Engraved with the figure of an antelope, it represented somebody's signature. The ring handed to Mordecai represented King Ahasuerus' signature, and conveyed the king's power of attorney. Likewise, Pharaoh gave his ring to Joseph as a symbol of conferring similar authority upon him (Gen. 41:42).

Once, King Ahasuerus handed over his authority too readily to an evil man, Haman. Again, he handed it over with startling readiness to Mordecai—but this time to a good man. The king didn't want the burdens of governing to distract him from his pleasures.

"And Esther set Mordecai over the house of Haman" (8:2).

As you grow in Christ, you discover it really is "more blessed to give than to receive" (Acts 20:35). What joy Esther must have found in giving the lavish estate of Haman to Mordecai! (See 5:11.) The estate would need managing. Esther endowed her foster father with wealth appropriate to his new position.

Thus God maneuvered His own into positions where they could act for His people. Esther, though in the king's presence, held no levers to exert force on the mighty king. A plaything in his life, she could only appeal.

"And Esther spake yet again before the king, and fell down at his feet, and besought him with tears to put away the mischief of Haman the Agagite, and his device that he had devised against the Jews" (8:3).

Notice the weapons she used: meekness—she fell at his feet; tears—she let her feelings show. Many times, modern family compromises can be worked out as each shows how he really feels.

One husband loved to fish—on ice, at dawn, on rivers, ponds, or lakes. His wife detested fishing. She could have gone along and gradually spoiled his joy in fishing. Or they could have fought out their differences bitterly. Instead, she set him free to fish. In return, she was free to travel now and then, and to involve herself in the church work she loved to do. In time, he joined her in the church work.

"And the king extended the golden scepter to Esther. So Esther arose and stood before the king. Then she said,

*'If it pleases the king and if I have found favor before him
and the matter seems proper to the king and I am pleasing in his sight, let it be written to revoke the letters
devised by Haman. . . . '''* (8:4-5, NASB)

Once again the king used the scepter—this time not to
spare her life, but to encourage her. Esther used not only
tears, but words. She kept on talking through her tears.
Who is moved by a woman who sulks, mopes, and
weeps, refusing to explain what's wrong?—expecting
you to guess?

Esther used tact. She put the blame for the horrible
edict on Haman, now dead. Again she gave the king
plenty of room to save face.

She used submission. She asked only for what he
might desire to give. She appealed positively to some
latent sense of justice in him. She wanted only what
might seem proper to him. The word in the Hebrew is
kasher. It's from the same root as the later Hebrew word
kosher, which means "sanctioned by Jewish law, ritu-
ally fit for use.

*"For how can I endure to see the evil that shall come
unto my people?"* (8:6)

Thus Esther continued what she had started. Before, she
had gotten only as far as her own life when the king
interrupted with his outburst against Haman (7:3-5).

Esther's tears were not for herself. She wept for her
people. Esther could not ultimately be separated from
her background, and neither can any of us. Sometimes
we accept some strange in-law relationship for the sake
of the one we love; also some strange loyalties. If we
truly love, we'll accept the whole person with all his
commitments, if possible. Esther showed patriotism

—concern for the group from which she had sprung. It was not a concern as large as the world, but one larger than herself.

"Then the King Ahasuerus said unto Esther the queen and to Mordecai the Jew, 'Behold, I have given Esther the house of Haman, and him they have hanged upon the gallows, because he laid his hand upon the Jews'" (8:7).

By way of encouragement, the king reminded Esther of how much he had already done. Then he told her what difficulties lay ahead.

"Write you also for the Jews, as it liketh you, in the king's name, and seal it with the king's ring: for the writing which is written in the the king's name, and sealed with the king's ring, may no man reverse" (8:8).

Unfortunately, the decree had already gone out, as Esther and Mordecai well knew. Persian kings tried to borrow from the gods some of the mystique of infallibility. Anything written into the laws of the Medes and Persians could not be altered.

To settle arguments, my father used to say to us as children, "Nope. Can't be done. It's written into the laws of the Medes and Persians." And we knew that was final.

The king found himself trapped in his own power. He couldn't simply undo the evil he had allowed in his name. Legislatures in democratic countries write laws, and they also repeal laws. Many parents make rules for their households, then find they must change the rules. Yet we all know people who regard themselves as infallible. They get themselves into endless miseries by refusing to shift and change. We all need others as correctives to ourselves. God knows we need to confess our sins daily, repent, and start over (1 John 1:8-10).

Ahasuerus couldn't wipe out the consequences of his wicked act, but he tried to counteract the foolish decree. Neither can we always wipe out consequences of our mistakes. Yet there is we can do much to counteract evil effects.

Two months and 10 days had passed since Haman's decree went out (8:9, compare 3:12). Once again, letters went to all 127 provinces extending from India to Ethiopia, written in languages the people could understand. This time Mordecai wrote in the king's name (8:10). Each letter was probably written on a piece of papyrus and tied up with a piece of string or ribbon. A lump of clay placed over the knot would be stamped with the king's signet ring.

"In them the king granted the Jews who were in each and every city the right to assemble and to defend their lives, to destroy, to kill, and to annihilate the entire army of any people or province which might attack them, including children and women, and to plunder their spoil, on one day in all the provinces of King Ahasuerus, the thirteenth day of the twelfth month (that is, the month Adar)" (8:11-12, NASB).

Haman had told the king the Jews were scattered, implying they were weak (3:8). But Mordecai got the Jews together to fast for Esther. Now he put through an edict allowing them to assemble to protect themselves.

Consider the effect in the time of Hitler if Jews had been given the right to unite. Suppose the government had given them permission to defend themselves against any who dared to attack. Far fewer would have died.

Israel as an assembled group of Jews has certainly proved able to defend itself. In the time of Hitler, Jews in the land of Israel marveled at how meekly those in Europe allowed themselves to be led off. One by one the dreaded Gestapo summoned individuals, usually in the night, to death or the concentration camp.

The edict of Mordecai for the Jews repeated the words of Haman's edict (3:13) against them.

"The written copy was made public law for all the people in every province; the Jews were to be ready on that day to avenge themselves on their enemies. So the messengers, riding the king's fast horses, went out speedily in keeping with the king's command; and the decree was issued also in the fortress city of Susa" (8:13-14, BECK).

Mordecai got the word out fast, using specially-bred royal horses. We all love to deliver good news. If you learn, say, of a job opportunity for someone who needs it, you get the word to him fast. You want him to have all possible time to prepare. You also want to ease his mind at the earliest possible moment.

"And Mordecai went out from the presence of the king in royal apparel of blue and white, and with a great crown of gold, and with a garment of fine linen and purple" (8:15).

Mordecai's new clothing reflected his new position. In Shakespeare's *Hamlet*, Polonius advises his son on dress: "Costly thy habit as thy purse can buy, but not express'd in fancy; rich, not gaudy; for the apparel oft proclaims the man" (Act I, Scene 3).

"And the city of Shushan rejoiced and was glad" (8:15).

Because Haman was dead? Because they respected Mordecai as a good man? Because they feared if the Jews suffered, they might be next? Because they simply didn't want to see any citizens unjustly treated? Probably for all of these reasons.

"The Jews had light, and gladness, and joy, and honor" (8:16).

Light, throughout the Bible, represents good as opposed to evil. It is a symbol of well-being. Jesus said, "I am the light of the world" (John 8:12). As we follow Him, we can walk in the Light all the time, through the darkest of circumstances.

The Christian has every reason to know gladness, because he's delivered from the sin that once bound him. Nothing feels as good as relief after pain, freedom after captivity, joy after grief. The Jews felt overwhelming relief from the pressure of dread. They were free from the sentence of death.

The Jews enjoyed honor. One of their own was now highest in the land, next to the king.

"And in every province, and in every city, whithersoever the king's commandment and his decree came, the Jews had joy and gladness, a feast and a good day" (8:17).

The tide of evil had turned. Ahead lay testing, uncertainty, and anxiety. Yet they rejoiced. If we waited till all problems were solved before we rejoiced, we'd never enjoy those little oases of celebration in our lives.

"And many of the people of the land became Jews; for the fear of the Jews fell upon them" (8:17).

Individuals from other cultures had come into Judaism, by persuasion: Ruth, the Moabite; Rahab, the Canaanite; Uriah the Hittite. But seldom before this had such a general movement toward Judaism taken place, unless you want to count the mixed multitude who went along with the Jews out of Egypt.

A Jewish commentator says that when the Jews saw the miracle of their deliverance, they accepted the Torah (the Pentateuch, Genesis to Deuteronomy) with great entuhsiasm. Seeing this, the Gentiles in Shushan gained new respect for the Torah and its teachings; thus they converted to Judaism.

In the time of Pharaoh, the magicians saw "the finger of God" in the 10 plagues. Likewise, in Persia non-Jews recognized some mysterious power acting in the Jews' behalf.

Can you do anything about evil? Should you? Or should you just sit and wait for God to intervene? The Bible says Christ will come again to deal with evil. He'll straighten everything out.

But in the meantime, God puts us into spots where we can act on His behalf. The Book of Esther shows how God combats evil through His own. James wrote, "Resist the devil, and he will flee from you" (James 4:7). Edmund Burke, an 18th-century English statesman, said, "The only thing necessary for the triumph of evil is for good men to do nothing."

11
How to Cope with Your Enemies

Have you noticed how God, at the climax of evil, can turn around bad events to work for your good?

Bart was a few months into a new and difficult pastorate. A man on the committee that called him said their church had tried almost everything to keep going, but nothing worked. "Now," he said, "we're going to try religion." The church members hadn't been able to keep up with their enormous building debt, and the small congregation faced the danger of losing its beautiful building.

We had problems at home too. The two-flat building in which we lived had changed hands, and the new owners moved in on the first floor. They decided with a name like Hess we had to be Nazis. We were the foreigners in an ethnic island of Chicagoland. We couldn't even speak their language. Therefore our landlord, and especially his wife, devoted themselves to making life miserable for us. Among other things, they provided us with 55 degrees (Fahrenheit) of heat in our upstairs flat. I was just home from the hospital with a new baby. A desperate housing shortage made moving impossible.

Some of the wonderful people in our church came over and tried to talk sense to them, in their mother tongue, but to no avail.

After a few months, we no longer even felt safe in that building. One day, when I returned from shopping, our landlady cursed and threatened me as I passed her door. Waving her arms, she almost pushed me backward down the stairs. I feared for the baby in my arms. That afternoon we moved out, storing our furniture in a loft of the church. I went home to mother, with two children. Bart rented a room near the church. Would we have to abandon that ministry simply because we could find no housing? But a great door was opening to us. Of course, there were many adversaries.

The next Sunday an officer of the church announced our plight to the congregation. A woman who rarely came to church "happened" to attend that day. She "happened" to have a flat coming vacant in a month. She "happened" to think it would bring "good luck" to have a minister living in her building.

But the rent loomed larger than we could possibly pay. The trustees decided to make up the difference, even though they didn't have the money at that time. To them it was an act of faith. We moved in and instructed our landlady later on the delicate matter of how much "luck" we could bring her.

The Lord turned those bad circumstances to the good for us. That church went on to become a strong Gospel church.

"Now in the twelfth month that is, the month Adar, on the thirteenth day of the same, when the king's commandment and his decree drew near to be put in execution, in the day that the enemies of the Jews hoped to

have power over them, (though it was turned to the con-
trary, that the Jews had rule over them that hated
them)" (9:1).

Throughout the Persian Empire, two opposing parties
stood ready to leap at each other's throats. Each held
legal right to kill and plunder the other. Ahasuerus had
decreed civil war; a race riot throughout the empire; a
gang rumble.

"The Jews gathered themselves together in their cities
throughout all the provinces of King Ahasuerus, to lay
hand on such as sought their hurt: and no man could
withstand them; for the fear of them fell upon all people"
(9:2).

Jews had spent the intervening nine months preparing. A
Jewish commentator says any Jew reading the account
would understand that "assembling" for war meant also
praying to God for success in battle.

Here, the Jews' action appears only defensive. Anyone who wanted to avoid being killed could simply have
stayed home that day. Yet often people prefer to gratify
their hatred even against their own best interests.

Seriously threatened, the Jews became mysteriously
invincible. A strange dread of them fell on the general
populace. As a similar dread fell on the peoples everywhere when Israel approached the Promised Land (Deut.
2:25). Remember, the Book of Esther forms a pattern for
subsequent Jewish history.

In 1967 Bart and I were in Iraq, visiting remains of
Babylon, Nineveh, and other places. We watched the
newspaper headlines, and read the articles vowing to
"push Israel into the Sea." Popular rhetoric declared
that Israel had no right to exist. We watched soldiers

gathering, saw troop trains moving toward the Israeli border. Nations totaling 40 to 50 million people were amassing against tiny Israel's almost 3 million. They believed Israel didn't stand a chance.

Five days before the war began, Britain ordered her subjects out of Iraq. We left too.

After the war began, it was all over in six days. No one could stand before Israel. A mysterious dread fell upon all the nations. It happened again in 1973, though that time Israel waited for the attack.

"Even all the princes of the provinces, the satraps, the governors, and those who were doing the king's business assisted the Jews, because the dread of Mordecai had fallen on them. Indeed, Mordecai was great in the king's house, and his fame spread throughout all the provinces; for the man Mordecai became greater and greater" (9:3-4, NASB).

From chapter 6 on to the end of the Book, Jews love to identify with Mordecai, who led his people to triumph over their enemies. We see their sense of community, of responsibility for each other. That quality persists. A beautiful young hygienist in Detroit explained how she was made to feel responsible for Israel's fortunes: "The synagogue has somebody that you can't say no to, like your mother-in-law, call you up and ask for what they feel you should contribute to the war needs in Israel. I had to give $1,100." That was a tenth of her year's salary—on top of what she already gave to the synagogue.

"Thus the Jews smote all their enemies with the stroke of the sword, and slaughter, and destruction, and did what they would unto those that hated them" (9:5).

Ugh. Here's where Christians really get troubled about the Book of Esther. "Does it really belong in the Bible?" they ask.

Remember the Book of Esther describes not how people should act, but how they do act. It recounts facts, neither blaming nor praising. It describes vividly how persecution gives birth to vindictiveness. The natural response to discrimination is unlimited revenge.

People even today operate on four different levels in dealing with enemies. First, a level that applied generally before Old Testament law came into being—unlimited retaliation. Lamech said to his wives, back in Genesis (4:23-24), "I have killed a man for wounding me; and a boy for striking me. If Cain is avenged sevenfold, then Lamech seventy-sevenfold." Seventy times seven meant no limit. A person paid back more than he got. The principle still operates in warfare when ten hostages are shot in response to the murder of one member of an occupying force.

Standards of retaliation in Esther have been superseded in theory, but not always in fact. Most of us have even experimented on different levels—at least in childhood.

One day, returning home from high school, I stood leaning over the kitchen table reading the funny paper. My brother walked by and snipped me with his fingernails in the obvious place. I grabbed a yardstick and chased him out the front door. As he ran down the steps, I cracked the yardstick over his head.

It was our last quarrel. After that, we became the best of friends. Somehow, when I heard that yardstick split, I saw how my retaliation would encourage his teasing. The persecuted, in retaliating, only lay the groundwork for the next persecution. I was responding on a pre-Old Testament level, returning worse treatment than I got.

Some people never outgrow that level. They spend their lives embroiled in endless conflict.

Mosaic Law limited retaliation to what was actually suffered. That represented a big advance: an eye for an eye, tooth for a tooth, life for a life. (See Ex. 21:24, or chapters 20—23; Deut. 19:19-21; Lev. 24:17.22.) This was the level of retaliation in Esther. They did to others as those others intended to do to them.

An intermediate level of no retaliation operates on the principle of, "'Vengeance is mine; I will repay,' saith the Lord'' (Rom. 12:19). Sometimes we feel virtuous if we simply refrain from hitting back. We avoid someone who has wronged us.

When I packed my belongings to leave that apartment, a friend helping me expressed her feelings. "My husband says if he had been treated the way you've been treated here, he'd pour acid down the pipes. In about three months the pipes would rot and the owners would never know what happened."

"Oh," I said, "I could never do anything like that. All I have to do to get out of this situation is move away. She has to live with herself." I knew enough to leave vengeance to God. But that was only a negative kind of goodness. In avoiding an enemy, I wasn't attaining any New Testament standard.

The highest level of how to treat an enemy was shown by Jesus. He told us to love our enemies and pray for those who despitefully use us (Matt. 5:43-48). I can't remember praying for that couple. And I think I was too scared to even think about loving them.

Later on in the church we learned about loving people who made themselves enemies to us. That's the real way to get relief from your enemies. Return good for evil. How often the person who behaves hatefully only needs more love and attention. If you can look beyond the difficult behavior, you will see his need. Then you can destroy him as your enemy for he becomes your friend. Paul said to act lovingly toward your enemy—feed him, give him a drink, overcome evil with good (Rom. 12:17-21). (For more details on this, see the author's book, *The Power of a Loving Church*.)

Retaliation leaves a sense of failure. It invites more retaliation. Returning good for evil yields the joy of victory. "Greater is He that is in you, than he that is in the world" (1 John 4:4).

"And in Shushan the palace the Jews slew and destroyed five hundred men, and . . . the ten sons of Haman the son of Hammedatha, the enemy of the Jews" (9:6-10).

Five hundred were killed in Susa the capital alone—the upper city. That many sought to attack the palace and destroy Esther, Mordecai, and other Jews. Mordecai was right that Esther could not hope to escape even in the palace (4:13).

Apparently, Haman infected his sons with his own hatred of Jews. All 10 pushed the attack forward. Parents carry an enormous responsibility for their children's attitudes. Yet a child need not perish blaming his parents. He can become responsible for his own attitudes. Haman's sons acted on their own responsibility, and suffered accordingly.

"But on the spoil laid they not their hand" (9:10).

The Jews retaliated, but not to the full limit the law allowed. They had legal right to seize all property of their enemies (8:11). They didn't. Perhaps the experience of Saul with the Amalekites echoed in their consciousness (1 Sam. 15). Saul lost the kingship because he kept the spoil of the Amalekites when God told him not to. By leaving the plunder for others, the Jews certainly encouraged Gentiles to help them.

"On that day the number of those that were slain in Shushan the palace was brought before the king. And the king said unto Esther the queen, 'The Jews have slain and destroyed five hundred men in Shushan the palace, and the ten sons of Haman; what have they done in the rest of the king's provinces? Now what is thy petition? And it shall be granted thee: or what is thy request further? And it shall be done'" (9:11-12).

King Ahasuerus obviously relished the reports of numbers killed. Perhaps the tally of corpses took him back to victorious times on the battlefield. You're shocked? But haven't you rejoiced with favorable war reports? Remember, various levels for treatment of enemies still operate in today's world, whatever our professed ideals.

"Then said Esther, 'If it please the king, let it be granted to the Jews which are in Shushan to do tomorrow also according unto this day's decree, and let Haman's 10 sons be hanged upon the gallows'" (9:13).

Horrors! Here gentle Esther, who wept and pled for her people, now wanted bitterest humiliation for their enemies. Displaying dead bodies was considered the lowest degradation. (See Deut. 21:22-23; Herodotus 3.125; 6.30; 7.238.)

And she wanted another day for killing! Again, this was war. In Esther's defense, remember the quarrel didn't start with the Jews. And she first wanted only to recall the decree against the Jews (8:5). No doubt she and Mordecai felt enemies still alive posed a dangerous threat. For security, the Jews needed another day.

Jews have always been a tiny minority in a society that sometimes tolerated, sometimes feared, sometimes admired, but frequently hated them. Jews have affected the society around them and the society around them has affected the behavior of Jews.

"And the king commanded it so to be done. . . . For the Jews that were in Shushan gathered themselves together on the fourteenth day also of the month Adar, and slew three hundred men in Shushan; but on the prey they laid not their hand" (9:14-15).

Four times the writer mentions that the Jews "assembled" (9:2, 15-16, 18). Three times he says they refused to enrich themselves with the spoil (9:10, 15-16).

"But the other Jews that were in the king's provinces gathered themselves together, and stood for their lives, and had rest from their enemies, and slew of their foes 75,000 but they laid not their hands on the prey" (9:16).

Commentators before the time of Hitler considered that number unlikely. Then Hitler actually did away with six million Jews, besides people of other races.

Estimates of the population of the Persian Empire vary from 73 million to 100 million. The Jews were only two or three million of that. Of those, probably 500,000 to 700,000 could bear arms. These might destroy 75,000 in battle throughout the entire Empire. Ahasuerus didn't grieve unduly over losing 1,000,000 men in his disastrous Greek campaign. What were 75,000 compared to that? And those 75,000 were not Persians. Persians were ranged throughout the Empire as a standing army. They stood with the governors, sympathetic to the Jews.

Those who attacked and would be killed represented subject nations. Their deaths would be no great grief to Persians.

At the beginning of the Book of Esther we don't see any general hatred of Jews. But we do see how race prejudice can start, how it can grow, and where it ends. Haman pointed Jews out as different, scattered, separate. Race prejudice grew as he appealed to greed and selfishness. Racialism ended in misery and death.

Before the time of Christ, the world knew little about pity. People did the most outrageous things to each other. They still do. But at least we know better now. Christ has taught us pity.

We know that the right way to fight is with spiritual weapons. "For we wrestle not against flesh and blood, but . . . against spiritual wickedness . . . . " (Eph. 6:12) Properly attired for war, we wear a helmet of salvation, an armor of truth, righteousness, peace. We fend off the attacks of the evil one by a shield of faith. And we attack with only one weapon—the sword of the Spirit, which is the Word of God (Eph. 6:13-18).

Studying the Book of Esther will help you to "fight" better. It helps you to understand the nature of the warfare. Satan has always wanted to destroy whomever represents God in the world. God in Christ shows us how best to counterattack.

12
How to Deal with Success

Success comes in many forms. To some, it means climbing a mountain. To others, it means winning a game, or breaking a record. Sometimes, it means winning an election, gaining a promotion, or achieving a prize. It may mean singing in a cantata, seeing a daughter graduate from college, seeing a loved one through an illness. Whatever success means to you, you want to know how to attain it, how to handle it when it comes.

Mordecai and the Jews enjoyed unusual success in the time of Esther. They won a war of self-defense. Mordecai gained the highest position in the great Empire of Ahasuerus. We've seen how he got there. How did the Jews and Mordecai handle success when it came?

"This was on the 13th day of the month of Adar, and on the 14th they rested and made it a day when they celebrated and were happy" (9:17, BECK).

After triumphing over enemies, the Jews reacted as people anywhere react when a war is won. They celebrated.

That's the first thing you do with success. If you've passed your exams, won the appointment, beat the opposing team, naturally you celebrate, usually with a feast; at least a dinner out. Every long struggle for success deserves a pause to savor it.

"But the Jews that were at Shushan assembled together on the thirteenth day thereof, and on the fourteenth thereof; and on the fifteenth day of the same they rested, and made it a day of feasting and gladness" (9:18).

Only in Susa did they carry on the struggle for another day. It was a necessary mop-up, they felt.

"Therefore the Jews of the villages, that dwelt in the unwalled towns, made the fourteenth day of the month Adar a day of gladness and feasting . . . . " (9:19)

Jews in the outlying areas enjoyed their day of rest before Jews in Susa laid down their arms. Therefore, to this day, you can find some Jews celebrating Purim for one day, others for two days. They celebrate this ancient victory in March, a month before Passover.

We all need rest. The Bible tells us how to meet that need. God "knoweth our frame; He remembereth that we are dust" (Ps. 103:14). He knows we can't struggle all the time.

Jesus said to come to Him, and He'd give us rest (Matt. 11:28-30). He also said, "Come away by yourselves to a lonely place and rest a while" (Mark 6:31, NASB). Jesus and his disciples had so many people coming and going that they didn't even have time to eat. We can learn from Jesus how to find peace in the midst of stress.

You can learn to relax with pressure before, behind,

and beside you. One businessman gets to work an hour early to enjoy an hour of prayer and Bible reading before others arrive. He thereby avoids the worst of the traffic. One doctor listens to Bible-study tapes as he drives and as he eats lunch at his desk. He creates his own little oasis of peaceful meditation. One minister unplugs his telephone at home for an hour between the day's work and the evening's activities. One housewife goes for a walk and looks at the changing seasons.

Jesus invited his close ones to a time of relaxation and intimate fellowship, with Himself and with each other. You can't face the opposition all the time. What relief you enjoy with family or friends when you've achieved some goal or other, against all odds!

"And Mordecai wrote these things" (9:20).

Some think from this notice that Mordecai wrote the whole Book of Esther. He may have, or he may have recorded the various facts, perhaps entered them into the Persian records. Perhaps someone else lifted them out and put them together. But if Mordecai wrote the account for the Persian records, that could explain some things.

While Persians allowed freedom of religion, they didn't encourage proselyting. Mordecai was vizier for the whole nation. He could well have felt he had no right to propagate his own faith in the official records.

The author, whoever he was, recounts only facts: no interpretations; no psychological speculations; no editorial comments; all totally objective. Only the *selection* of facts screams the power of God on every page—to him who has the eye of faith. Likewise, the beauties of nature cry "God" to the believer. To many unbelievers, nature speaks only of blind chance.

"And he sent letters to all the Jews who were in all the provinces of King Ahasuerus, both near and far, obliging them to celebrate . . . annually, because on those days the Jews rid themselves of their enemies, and it was a month which was turned for them from sorrow into gladness and from mourning into a holiday; that they should make them days of feasting and rejoicing" (9:20-22, NASB).

The second thing to do with success is to remember. Remember the struggles that brought you to where you are. Remember the terrible job you had that makes the present one easy by contrast. Remember your anxiety about passing from 11th grade into 12th grade. You wondered then if you could ever meet the new challenges. You did. Each challenge met gives courage for the next one. Remember to help your child taste the fruits of success. Help him get into the habit of succeeding.

Remember the sorrows survived. "You don't think it's possible now," wrote an older woman to one whose mother had just died, "but in time Christ can and will fill the empty place." He did. You grow with each difficulty overcome.

This feat of rejoicing climaxes the feasts of the Book of Esther. To a Jew, remembering meant recalling all of God's deliverances, starting with His deliverance from Egypt, which Jews celebrate with the yearly Passover feast. When God released the Israelites from Egypt, He worked many obvious miracles (see Ex. 5-14). In Esther, God's deliverance seemed only a matter of everyday court intrigues, as His deliverances in the future would seem time and again the outcome of ordinary events.

God can turn the course of events upside down. In this

case He did. We learn from the Book of Esther that He controls all happenings, small and large.

Remembering, for us, means remembering how God brought us to the present moment. We all have reasons to celebrate.

The Bible gives a big place to "joy" (9:22). "Rejoice always" (1 Thes. 5:16; see also 1 Peter 1:8; John 15:11; Phil. 4:4). Rejoice when God gives you success; rejoice also when He gives you failure. By failure He has taught you one more way not to do something. It may prove an important step on the road to success. He has promised to those who love Him and accept His way that all things work together for good (Rom. 8:28).

"Sending portions of food to one another . . . " (9:22, NASB)

The third thing to do with success is share it. Share it with those who have helped make it possible. A victory celebration on election night includes the humblest workers. We can't really enjoy ourselves until we have shared. All Jews suffered together the trauma of dread. All shared in the struggle against common enemies. Sending choice portions of food to friends meant reminding each other of Jewish togetherness.

"And gifts to the poor . . . " (9:22)

This was a very Hebrew touch to the celebration. Moses exhorted the Israelites to include in their holy feasts not only family and servants and priests, but also strangers, orphans, and widows (Deut. 16:11, 14; see also Neh. 8:10, 12; 1 John 3:17). Jewish gifts to charity, usually money, peak at the Purim season.

A Jewish short story about Purim describes the subtle

complications of these exchanges. Certain relationships call for precise exchanges. In some cases a Jewish woman would be very careful not to send too much. She must not put the other person in the position of a charity case. On the other hand, the poor person receiving a large gift would know he must not attempt to reciprocate. That would rob the giver of the satisfaction of having sent his portion to the poor.

We enjoy our Christmas celebration more keenly when we have shared with the needy. We too remind ourselves of kinship ties with even gift exchanges.

"And the Jews undertook to do as they had begun, and as Mordecai had written unto them" (9:23).

The Purim holidays began spontaneously. Mordecai encouraged what was already taking place.

"Because Haman the son of Hammedatha, the Agagite, the enemy of all the Jews, had devised against the Jews to destroy them, and had cast Pur, that is, the lot, to consume them and to destroy them. But . . . the king . . . commanded . . . " (9:24-25).

God worked through that lot to turn Haman's plans around. Haman, in turning to the lot, trusted his gods to set a propitious day. But our God, totally in command, controlled the lot. If the lot had fallen on an earlier date, the Jews would have been wiped out. It fell in the latest month possible, giving time for Mordecai to exhort Esther, Esther to appeal to the king, the king to destroy Haman and exalt Mordecai, and Mordecai to instruct the Jews. So what better name for the total celebration than Purim? The word Purim is based on the Persian word "pur" (the lot) with a Hebrew plural added.

"Wherefore they called these days Purim after the name of Pur" (9:26).

Haman's sin of pride, with which his own troubles started, spread to affect his family, his nation, and the empire. Likewise, the fall of Lucifer began with the sin of pride (Isa. 14:12-17; Ezek. 28:11-19). Lucifer set himself up to equal God. Cast out of heaven, he became the adversary, Satan, who would trouble the people of God throughout history. The Bible tells us he won't cause trouble forever (Rev. 20:10). "God is the judge: He putteth down one, and setteth up another" (Ps. 75:7). We learn from Haman how not to succeed.

"The Jews ordained, and took upon them . . . so as it should not fail, that they would keep these two days . . . every year" (9:27).

The celebration of Purim naturally appealed more strongly to Jews scattered among the heathen than to those in the Land. But by the time of the Maccabees, the second century before Christ, it was celebrated in Palestine (2 Maccabees 15:36). Josephus, a Jewish historian in the first century after Christ, wrote of Purim: "In like manner the Jews that were in Shushan gathered themselves together, and feasted on the fourteenth day, and that which followed it; whence it is, that even now all the Jews that are in the habitable earth keep these days festivals, and send portions to one another" (Josephus *Antiquities of the Jews* 11.6).

Purim, of course, isn't one of the holy feasts ordained by Moses (Lev. 23). It's an historical observance, a spontaneous folk celebration like our Fourth of July, or Thanksgiving.

Throughout history Jews have never observed Purim

in the same solemn way as Passover, or Yom Kippur, the Day of Atonement. The only religious aspect of Purim is going to the synagogue to hear the Megillah (scroll) read, as Jews call the Book of Esther.

To Jews, the Book of Esther stands second only to the Pentateuch (Genesis to Deuteronomy). Maimonides, the most celebrated Jewish scholar of the Middle Ages, said that in the days of Messiah the only Scriptures left would be the Law and the Scroll (Esther). More manuscript copies of Esther exist than of any other book in the Old Testament.

Esther has lived because enemies of the Jews would not let it die. Its popularity increased in proportion to persecution suffered. It has become to Jews the most popular and well-known of all biblical books.

Persecution of Jews started early. Papyri tell us of Egyptian hostility to Jews at Elephantine back in the fifth century B.C. But for a chance find, we'd know nothing about it. Future such finds may tell us more about what went on in the Persian Empire in the time of Esther. To date, we know little more than what the Book of Esther tells us.

Jews suffered under Antiochus Epiphanes in the second century before Christ. Throughout the Middle Ages, civil authorities and church alike terrified and tortured Jews. They were banished, imprisoned, and robbed of their possessions. Spain used to take the lead; then Russia, Lithuania, Poland, and Rumania stepped forward with their pogroms.

In our civilized 20th century, Germany outdid all predecessors. A former Jewish judge who escaped from Nazi Germany was living in Paris. He said, "Not because of what we have done, but because of who we are, we are to be destroyed. We are regarded as bugs. How do you treat a bug?" The dignified ex-judge paused to

grind an imaginary bug into the pavement with his foot.
"You destroy it."

The Book of Esther gave comfort and encouragement
to Jews in medieval ghettos, to Jews in modern Germany's concentration camps, to Jews wherever they suffered even petty discriminations.

When Esther is read in the synagogue, the service is
not solemn and quiet like most Jewish services. Whenever the reader mentions Haman's name, the audience
stamps its feet and makes noises to boo Haman. Historically, celebrants have concocted all kinds of noisemakers. They would shake stones in metal or whirl wooden
noisemakers to make a whining or a clacking sound.
Sometimes, they wrote the name of Haman on the soles
of their shoes, then stamped to rub it out. Children entered into the noisemaking with special gusto.

Too often, the violent expressions really gave vent to
hatred of the current or local Haman. For downtrodden
Jews it was a psychological safety valve that was politically safe. Sometimes, they burned Haman in effigy.

*"And that these days should be remembered and kept
throughout every generation, every family, every province, and every city; and that these days of Purim should
not fail from among the Jews, nor the memorial of them
perish from their seed"* (9:28).

The feast of Purim celebrated today forms a living link
with the events of Esther. If you visit Tel Aviv, Israel on
the 14th and 15th of Adar (generally in March), you'll
find a super celebration of Purim: banners, parades,
floats, feasts, parties, dancing in the streets, masquer-
ades, and Purim plays. The Book of Esther is read in the
synagogues. It's also broadcast by loudspeakers in the
streets for people who can't get in. Jews come from all

over the world to experience Purim in Tel Aviv, the all-Jewish city.

Throughout the world, if you go to a synagogue in your own city the morning of Purim, or possibly the evening before, you'll find Esther read. In Jewish homes afterward, families gather. Work and business is allowed—it's not a holy day. Shops in Jewish neighborhoods carry special Purim pastries, especially the "hamantaschen." These three-cornered pastries or sweet rolls contain poppy seeds and honey, or prune filling. The pastries are supposed to represent Haman's hat—or the three people at Esther's banquet. Some say the poppy seeds represent Jews, "like the dust of the earth in number" (see Gen. 13:16).

Purim has been a time for unrestrained merrymaking. Tradition decrees it proper to drink wine until the celebrant can't distinguish between "Blessed be Mordecai" and "Cursed be Haman." Naturally, some Jews deplore such abandon, and don't go to any such extremes. Like any folk festival, the Purim celebration constantly grows and changes with every generation.

"Then Esther the queen . . . wrote . . . to confirm . . ." (9:29).

She added her authority to that of Mordecai. Together they sent letters to Jews in all the provinces with "words of peace and truth" (9:30).

Mordecai and Esther together added "the rules for themselves and their descendants with regard to fasting and weeping" (9:31, BECK). To this day, a complete celebration of Purim includes fasting the day before. The fast recalls Esther's fast before she went in to appeal to the king. Naturally, the fast makes the feast all the more enjoyable.

"And the decree of Esther confirmed these matters of Purim; and it was written in the book" (9:32).

The name of Esther occurs 55 times—more than the name of any other woman in the Bible, more times even than the name of Sarah, wife of Abraham.

What book is referred to in 9:32? Probably the Persian records mentioned in 2:23, 6:1, and 10:2. Recording Esther's decree showed its historical significance.

The fourth thing to do with success is to fulfill all your responsibilities. Work at the political office to which you have been elected; faithfully attend rehearsals for the solo part you've been asked to sing; find out and perform all the duties of the church office you have accepted. It's so easy to enjoy the advantages but neglect the obligations of any desirable position.

"Now King Ahasuerus laid a tribute on the land and the coastlands of the sea" (10:1, NASB).

As high executive officer, Mordecai had to raise money to run the government. He found a better way than killing and plundering Jews. Mordecai apparently persuaded Ahasuerus to tax everyone equally. Numerous reliefs at Persepolis from the time of Darius and Xerxes show deputations bearing taxes from far provinces. They carry gold dust in jars, war axes, a wild ass, an elephant tusk, and many other items. Innumerable remains of great building projects testify to the greatness and power of Xerxes.

"And all the acts of his power and of his might, and the declaration of the greatness of Mordecai, whereunto the king advanced him, are they not written in the Book of the Chronicles of the kings of Media and Persia?" (10:2)

The author ends, as he began, with a description of Xerxes' wealth and power. If the account hadn't been historical, the writer wouldn't refer his readers to well-known records.

"For Mordecai the Jew was next unto King Ahasuerus, and great among the Jews, and accepted of the multitude of his brethren, seeking the wealth of his people, and one speaking peace to all his seed" (10:3).

The fifth thing to do with success is to use it for the benefit of others. Jews have suffered many Hamans, but "He that keepeth Israel shall neither slumber nor sleep" (Ps. 121:4). God has raised up many Mordecais. Many Jews have occupied high places in government, and positions of influence.

Mordecai gained his success through humility, principle, courage, and perseverance. He showed himself more anxious to deserve the king's favor than to enjoy it.

Mordecai was an important person in the drama. He stood at the center of practically all the action, a vehicle for God's purposes in the world.

You too can be God's vehicle in your generation.